Pedagogy, not Policing

Also published by The Graduate School Press of Syracuse University

Using Writing to Teach

Interrupting Heteronormativity
*Lesbian, Gay, Bisexual and Transgender Pedagogy
and Responsible Teaching at Syracuse University*

Building Pedagogical Curb Cuts
*Incorporating Disability in the University
Classroom and Curriculum*

Building Community
*Stories and Strategies for Future Learning
Community Faculty and Professionals*

PEDAGOGY, NOT POLICING

Positive Approaches to Academic Integrity at the University

Edited by

Tyra Twomey
Holly White
and Ken Sagendorf

The Graduate School Press
Syracuse University

Library of Congress Cataloging-in-Publication Data

Pedagogy, not policing : positive approaches to academic integrity at the university / edited by Tyra Twomey, Holly White, and Ken Sagendorf.
    p. cm.
  Includes bibliographical references.
  Summary: "Considers various issues related to academic integrity in the college/university setting"~ Provided by publisher.
  ISBN-13: 978-0-9777847-4-5
  ISBN-10: 0-9777847-4-6
  1. Cheating (Education)~United States. 2. College students~United States~Conduct of life. 3. Universities and colleges~Corrupt practices~United States. 4. Education, Higher~Moral and ethical aspects~United States. I. Twomey, Tish Eshelle. II. White, Holly, 1973- III. Sagendorf, Ken, 1973-
  LB3609.P36 2008
  378.1'98~dc22

                          2008054237

For more information about this publication, please contact:

The Graduate School
423 Bowne Hall
Syracuse University
Syracuse, NY 13244

gradschpdprograms.syr.edu
gradsch.syr.edu

Manufactured in the United States of America

Contents

Acknowledgments

THE EDITORS WOULD like to express their appreciation to all who contributed to the completion of this book.

We would like to share our gratitude to our advisory board of faculty, staff, and administrators: Ernest Hemphill, David Bozak, Elleta Calahan, Rebecca Howard, Judy O'Rourke, Abby Kasowitz-Scheer, Barbara Fought, David Potter, Martin Sage, Stacey Lane Tice, and Michael Olivette.

We owe special recognition to Stacey Lane Tice, the Future Professoriate Program, and the Graduate School of Syracuse University for their continuing support of unique pedagogical projects and their support of doctoral students.

Special thanks to Craig Martin for all of his work on this project and Glenn Wright for seeing it to completion at the end.

Finally, we sincerely thank all of the authors who answered the call for pieces and were patient in the process. We hope you find the product to be as wonderful as we do.

—Tyra, Holly, and Ken

Foreword

Patrick Drinan

THE ACADEMIC INTEGRITY movement began in earnest in the early 1990s when Professor Donald McCabe of Rutgers University and a few like-minded individuals from across the country started a series of annual conferences that led to the formation of the Center for Academic Integrity. Professor McCabe had been doing massive surveys of the incidence of student cheating in American higher education.

Various student affairs administrators also were interested in diffusion of best practices in managing what was rightly perceived to be the growing problem of student academic dishonesty in the academy. The fortuitous combination of Professor McCabe's research and efforts to spread best practices led to a national, and now international, effort to promote student academic honesty and engage a wide public discourse about how to manage the issues associated with student academic dishonesty.

This discourse has increased its profile over the last 20 years, and many of the best colleges and universities in the country have become willing to address the issues instead of sweeping them under the rug.

This takes courage. It also takes coordination.

But why pay attention to student academic dishonesty when there are so many pressing concerns and distractions on our campuses? The answer comes in advancing the essential missions of teaching and research by increasing the radius of trust in our academic communities, both in the classroom and beyond. Effective and responsive teaching lowers the incidence of cheating and increases our confidence when determining merit. Even in research universities, faculty overwhelmingly report that teaching gives them most of their career satisfaction. But faculty cannot promote academic honesty—or reduce academic dishonesty— if they act like Robinson Crusoes on the desert islands of the classroom. We need to learn from each other, support each other, and know that our institutions value these efforts. The editors and authors should be commended for the exercise of diligence and clarity of thought exhibited in this volume. It is another important step in a more robust definition of professionalism for all of us as teachers. It shows that we not only know we can do better, but are prepared to do so; this a very good sign.

Pedagogy, not Policing

Editors' Introduction

Tyra Twomey, Holly White, and Ken Sagendorf

ACADEMIC INTEGRITY is not a new topic in higher education. Honor codes and academic dishonesty are familiar concepts for guiding scholarly conduct. But why the emphasis on "integrity" instead of dishonesty, plagiarism, or just plain cheating?

"Integrity" often refers to one's character. At the surface, it may seem easy to differentiate between people and actions with integrity and those without. And the public trust placed in academe would indicate that integrity in higher education should be at a high level. We expect our scholars, teachers, researchers, and leaders to be exemplary not only in knowledge but also in character and behavior—a premise that accords with the public outcry we encounter when integrity violations at the academy are made known.

Though the issues around integrity in higher education are not news, this topic has received a marked increase in attention as accountability in higher education has become more important. This increase can be understood in several ways. One could note that as our society focuses more and more on standardization and certification, educational institutions at all levels are under increasing pressure to communicate their methods and goals to governmental and corporate bodies. While this is one way to read the situation, another is to take note that institutions are having to become more transparent about the policies and practices that consolidate power. We would argue that this give-and-take between higher education and the public regarding the standards espoused at colleges and universities is overall a healthy development. The need for the "Ivory Tower" to respond to the call for thinking itself in its social context and to take less for granted is at the core of the philosophy behind the liberal institution and, arguably, higher education as a modern cultural value.

One method of reflecting these values implicit in higher education is to institutionalize them through policy. For example, the Syracuse University Academic Integrity policy lays its foundation on "a commitment to the values of honesty, trustworthiness, fairness, and respect." We would agree that these are worthy values, and that their converses are not so. This agreement leads us, as educators, to feeling offended when someone lacks commitment to any one of these values. That reaction is probably at the core of why many think of academic integrity violations as repudiations of these values and why many think of academic integrity itself as an issue of enforcement. It is a matter of protecting what we hold dear.

This book explores academic integrity using a different approach. Instead of seeking out ways to identify, catch, and punish those who cheat or plagiarize, this book explores what universities, instructors, and students can do to create an environment that promotes honesty, trust, and respect.

This book is a product of the Future Professoriate Program (FPP) of the Syracuse University Graduate School. FPP has been responsible for identifying topics at Syracuse University, and in higher education more generally, ripe for rich examination and productive work toward making changes in approaches and practices. It has provided funding and direction to staff and students to not only collaborate in the creation of these works but also gain experience by editing and producing such volumes—experience that many of us will build upon as we pursue careers in higher education. We were invited to be editors by FPP because our graduate work and professional interests involve academic integrity, teaching, faculty life, interdisciplinarity, and the role of higher education in society.

This book is organized into four sections. The first asks us to reconsider our assumptions and basic definitions so as to think critically about both what we mean when we use the term academic integrity and what the implications of that thinking are for ourselves, our institutional practices, and the students we teach. The second draws attention to the particular position of the graduate student in the academy as a student—one hovering or oscillating between the poles of what is often described as a teacher/student binary—and the unique pressures for defining and practicing "integrity" that this position entails. The third section, titled "The People Behind the Policies," offers elements ranging from personal reflections to programmatic descriptions, contributed by a range of writers including an undergraduate student, a TA, a faculty member, and two administrators from different campus offices, each sharing experience and advice from a localized perspective. Finally, the fourth section offers practical strategies for instructors and TAs to apply so as to promote a climate of integrity in their classrooms.

The primary goal of educators is not eliminating dishonesty, it is educating. And with this goal in focus, we can accept that the factors and pressures that lead to scholars *at any level* misrepresenting their work are not going away. As educators, while we may visualize a utopian environment of consistent, honest scholastic performance, we do better to recognize that such a pure place is not possible and to make choices in our pedagogies that move away from policing towards practicing the behaviors we say we value. We hope that this book inspires you to form your own pedagogical style in promoting academic integrity in your classrooms. But we also hope that, as you encounter familiar issues and suggestions, you will feel affirmed as a educator. It is good to remember that in many ways, promoting academic integrity is not something new we have to conform to: it is what happens naturally whenever we are active learners and thoughtful educators.

I
THEORY IN PRACTICE
WHAT IS ACADEMIC INTEGRITY, AND WHAT ARE
ITS IMPLICATIONS FOR TEACHERS AND STUDENTS?

———————————

AT FIRST GLANCE, the question above may seem over-familiar, if not facile, and its answers obvious: academic integrity is doing your own work, not cheating, "playing fair." If everybody practiced it, school would run the way it "should." When not everybody does, we have problems, and there are punishments to mete out and cheaters to catch. But such a simplistic appraisal overlooks the real complexity of both the notion of academic integrity and its implications for us all, which can be easily seen if we stop to interrogate the assumptions the simple answers take for granted. Ask, for example, what makes "academic" integrity a separate concept from "integrity" itself—why don't we just have policies asking students to do everything with integrity? Is that outside our jurisdiction? What *is* our jurisdiction? Ask what "integrity" means in the first place, and why, if its opposites in most academic integrity policies are words such as "cheating," "plagiarism," and "academic *dishonesty*," we don't just call it "academic honesty"?

Ask why doing one's "own" work is culturally superior to working collaboratively—and ask whether or not this is universally true. Ask why it *matters* whether or not students cheat, if they also learn, and if as teachers our job is just to teach them. Ask what the purpose is of seeking an undergraduate or graduate education—and if you think of such possible answers as career opportunities, field advancement, or job experience, ask whether these are more likely to come to students who can most convincingly demonstrate that they have learned from their coursework or to students who have the best credentials—and the highest GPA. And while you're at it, ask about grading curves, "culling" classes,[1] and interdepartmental funding wars over enrollment statistics. Ask who benefits from teaching and learning "with integrity"—not only from the perspective of a humanistic belief in the value of education, but also through a consideration of the economies of grades, degree requirements, scholarship stipulations, enrollment statistics, part-time vs. full-time instructors' salaries, overly full schedules, and competitive job markets.

The pieces in this section take on these difficult questions, placing the academy and its expectations of its teachers and students under tough theoretical scrutiny. David Horacek examines the nature of knowledge-making to see how the concept of "academic integrity" has evolved as a matter of necessity. Amy Roache-Fedchenko investigates academic integrity as a climate to promote rather than a set of practices or lapses. Ben Lovett asks what it is about educators' approaches that makes cheating seem to some students like a *type* of "fair play"; Jim Pangborn examines the ways the tasks we ask of writers set them up to plagiarize as an act of panic. Mike Murphy provides a critical examination of the commodification of education in today's economies, and Matthew Bertram challenges our basic cultural understandings of textual ownership and "originality." Then, going further, each writer brings his or her thought-provoking reflection into the realm of the concrete, sharing learned experience to suggest what can be done in real classrooms to address this complexity in ways that recognize students' rationality and autonomy and invite their participation in making and partaking of a shared academic culture of integrity.

Notes

1. This is a term heard in circulation at a large state school offering a wide array of degrees in science and engineering fields whose programs of study began with a series of large, lecture-based introductory courses, sometimes seating as many as 400 students per lecture, the grades for which courses were determined solely by multiple-choice tests graded on curves and designed to be difficult. Large numbers of students never made it past these introductory courses, and thus the "herds" were "culled" down to more reasonable numbers of only the strongest students—or at least those best at passing multiple-choice tests in crowded rooms. Other institutions have other ways of referring to this not uncommon practice, but likely none as metaphorically vivid.

Academic Integrity and Intellectual Autonomy

David Horacek

WHEN ACADEMICS bring up academic integrity, it is usually a prelude to telling our students that they are not allowed to cheat or plagiarize. Thanks to the realities of teaching, our own reflections about academic integrity tend to focus on the important practical work of deterring cheaters, as well as catching those who would not be deterred. In this chapter I want to investigate some rather more philosophical questions about academic integrity. What is it? What good is it? What makes its codes obligatory? My answers to these questions suggest that the most basic justification for academic integrity is one not usually discussed among educators, nor is it described to students. I argue that it is possible, and not unusual, for dishonest academic work to be produced without cheating, plagiarizing, or doing anything that universities forbid. This sort of dishonest work is wrong for the same reason that cheating is, insofar as both violate core principles of academic integrity. We educators should do our best to eliminate all failures of academic integrity in students, both the forbidden and the allowed, because both interfere with the development of a student's intellectual autonomy.

Every university publication on academic integrity that I have surveyed declares academic dishonesty to be forbidden. Here is one representative paragraph, which comes from a document published by Purdue University called "Academic Integrity: A Guide for Students":

Purdue prohibits "dishonesty in connection with any University activity. Cheating, plagiarism, or knowingly furnishing false information to the University are examples of dishonesty." [Part 5, Section III-B-2-a, *University Regulations*] Furthermore, the University Senate has stipulated that "the commitment of acts of cheating, lying, and deceit in any of their diverse forms (such as the use of substitutes for taking examinations, the use of illegal cribs, plagiarism, and copying during examinations) is dishonest and must not be tolerated. Moreover, knowingly to aid and abet, directly or indirectly, other parties in committing dishonest acts is in itself dishonest" [University Senate Document 72-18, December 15, 1972]. (Akers, 2003)

Universities that provide more elaborate descriptions of academic integrity will often mention reasons to justify their administrative policies. For example, the academic integrity policy of Syracuse University argues that cheating "is unfair to other community members who do not cheat, because it devalues efforts to learn, to teach, and to conduct research" (Preamble).

Universities set out to accomplish two important tasks with their academic integrity policies: the first is to describe the nature and scope of academic integrity while (in some cases) giving reasons why it should be respected. The second is to state clearly what sorts of activities are forbidden. I believe these are two very different tasks, but because they are almost always done within the same document, policy authors tend to conflate them. Doing so leads to two conceptual mistakes: one of them, made in the Purdue document, is to correctly describe academic integrity as avoiding "dishonesty in connection with any University activity" but then say something false—namely, that all such dishonesty is forbidden. In fact, neither Purdue nor any other academic institution would forbid everything that falls under this broad category. Though it describes cheating, plagiarism, and furnishing false information merely as examples of dishonesty in academic work, these specific types of dishonesty are de facto the only ones that are banned.

The more common and conceptually more pernicious mistake is to begin with a detailed list of the academic activities that are banned (cheating, plagiarism, falsified data), and then go on to suggest that academic integrity is achieved if these specific perils are avoided.

To undo these tempting mistakes, I want to first investigate which activities a university ought to ban, and why. After this, I undertake a separate investigation of academic integrity. Bringing these results together will reveal a more complicated relationship than university policies would probably care to discuss. But my goal in this chapter is to improve our understanding, not our policies.

First, I consider the question of how university policies on academic integrity are justified. Insofar as these policies focus on where students ought not trespass, they may appear to be nothing more than institutional rules, sanctioned perhaps by long tradition. If understood as an institutional code of conduct, the rules of academic integrity are conceptually easy to make sense of. Each student sorority, for example, also has its own code of conduct. In joining the sorority, the student acknowledges that she accepts this code. Perhaps joining the university involves a similar acknowledgment.

But clearly, the two cases are not analogous. The code of a sorority may, after all, include many *arbitrary* restrictions on behavior, such as prohibitions on certain outfits and foods. The requirements of academic integrity are, and are clearly meant to be understood as, non-arbitrary. Treating the codes as brute rules with punitive consequences may come close to how many undergraduates understand the matter, but for our purposes it is inadequate. At best, it explains why it is in the interest of students to follow the codes, but does not explain why these codes are right, and why they should be internalized and revered.

Describing its opposite as "academic dishonesty" suggests that academic integrity is obligatory because dishonesty is morally wrong. Syracuse University uses of the word "unfair" to describe cheating, suggesting a moral weight behind the university's codes. While cheating is clearly dishonest, this by itself not does not justify a ban. For one thing, it is unclear whether all dishonesty is immoral. Certain falsehoods and omissions of truth often expedite sensitive collaborations and harm neither the liar nor the victim. This point is relevant here because students who are caught cheating often wonder what the big deal is about appropriate citations and independent work. Many assignments that we require of them

> *There is no university prohibition on bullshitting, yet there is one on cheating. Both are obviously dishonest. Why is it not arbitrary that one sort of dishonesty is tolerated while the other is forbidden?*

seem to them like exercises and mere formalities, the very sort of territory where "white lies" rarely do harm. There is no university prohibition on bullshitting,[1] yet there is one on cheating. Both are obviously dishonest. Why is it not arbitrary that one sort of dishonesty is tolerated while the other is forbidden?

Even if all dishonesty were immoral, why does the university mandate adherence to certain moral principles and not others? I claim the university does not have sufficient license to legislate any moral principles *simply because they are moral*. (If it did, *all* moral principles would require legislating.) Legislating the codes of academic integrity requires an independent rationale. In the extended argument below, I attempt to reconstruct this rationale, but also to call attention to aspects of academic integrity that are outside the scope of legislation. Once more is said about these unlegislated aspects of academic integrity, I will examine its role in the education of students, concluding that it plays a privileged role in their intellectual maturation.

All Researchers Form a Community, One That Defines Itself Through Its Adherence to the Code of Academic Integrity

Students of medicine, law, carpentry, and many other praxis-oriented fields understand themselves as initiates to a community of practitioners. College students typically do not. For many reasons, however, they should. They are initiates to the *community of researchers*.

Since communities of practitioners typically follow certain codes of conduct, a part of the initiation into any community will require the initiates to internalize its codes. Future doctors, for example, must not only understand the Hippocratic Oath, but also embrace it as the necessary principle that must bind their conduct as doctors. This traditional set of codes has much in common with the codes of academic integrity. Adherence to each is *required* within its respective discipline. Each is supported by moral considerations. Each is a code that defines an institution and a community. In each case, personal internalization of the codes of the community is necessary for membership.

Someone who is trained as a doctor but does not abide by the Hippocratic Oath is not acting as a doctor, because she does not share in the primary priorities of medicine. For example, she may decide that one of her patients is immoral and deserves to suffer, so she uses her knowledge to cause him suffering. We can invent situations in which this sort of behavior might be understandable or even justifiable, but what is clear is that even if she is acting justifiably, she is not acting as a doctor. There are excellent reasons for the community of doctors to abhor anything that tempts them to make exceptions to their Hippocratic Oath. I will not list these reasons here. I bring up the topic only for the sake of drawing an analogy: the codes of academic integrity are to the community of inquirers what the Hippocratic Oath is to the community of medical practitioners.

It would be strange to call the Hippocratic Oath a code of honor, as though it would distinguish the honorable doctors from the rest. The oath does not outline a standard of excellence or virtue; it only sets out the *barest minimum* of what is required of a doctor. Yet it has been suggested that the code of academic integrity should be understood as a code of honor. I think this is wrong. As in the case of medicine, the code of academic integrity doesn't distinguish the honorable researchers from the rest. For that matter, the code also doesn't distinguish the honorable students from the rest. The code of academic integrity defines the ground floor of what is acceptable, whereas acting by any code of *honor* would clearly require going above and beyond the barest minimum of acceptability. Therefore, the code of academic integrity is not a code of honor for researchers and students, and it is misleading to describe it as such.

I noted earlier the impression left by many university policies that academic integrity is achieved merely by avoidance of certain banned activities like cheating. The same mistake in the medical analogy would be this: thinking that being true to the Hippocratic Oath requires simply the avoidance of malpractice. No one would realistically think this, because we understand that only a small subset of the responsibilities in the Hippocratic Oath are explicitly legislated as bans of the sort that would trigger malpractice charges. The same mistake is easier

> *The code of academic integrity defines the ground floor of what is acceptable, whereas acting by any code of* honor *would clearly require going above and beyond the barest minimum of acceptability.*

to make in the academic case, though it is no less a mistake. There is more to following a community-defining code than merely the avoidance of some forbidden activities.

Why the Academy Needs the Code of Academic Integrity

There is no alternative to academic integrity, no standard perhaps less honorable or chivalrous, that will allow the community of researchers to accomplish its goals. It is *required* for productive interactions among researchers. This indispensability is the extra-moral component needed to justify *legislating* aspects of this code.[2]

Young people may not immediately appreciate the indispensability of academic integrity to getting research done. Because it is sometimes introduced as an honor code, some may suspect that academic integrity is a quaint idealism. Others might find it noble in principle, but also suspect that, like the wigs of English barristers, strict codes of academic integrity are vestigial, ornamental, and potentially cumbersome. Might we not be better served by a bit of flexibility? The answer is no. Consider a society in which researchers feel no compulsion to abide by the codes of academic integrity. Imagine, for example, that various corporations each support a flock of academics whose job is to act in the interest of their employer. They release studies vindicating the superiority and safety of the products of their benefactors, while casting doubt on the products of their competitors. They extol the virtues of a certain ideology, while sweeping its shortcomings under the rug. They make up titles and invent citations, while taking credit for the work of others. In general, they feel no compulsion to be sincere in their work.

One obvious cost of this arrangement is that we laypeople wouldn't have anyone to trust. How would we make informed decisions about what policies we should support, what products were safe, or what diets were effective, if every available source felt free to make things up? But the problem would be more serious than just a lack of information for laypeople: experts would be in exactly the same situation. This sort of an intellectual climate would require every individual researcher to personally confirm the conclusions of others, since their accuracy could not be assumed. The situation would quickly become unmanageable, and no such system could survive for long before groups of researchers decided to pool their resources so that each one would not individually have to duplicate every result. Pooling resources in this way would absolutely require that the cooperating scientists be sincere with one another. If they were to put their cooperation agreement into the form of a contract, it would not only pledge a "formal" honesty of correct attribution, absence of plagiarism, etc., but would also forbid the researchers from bullshitting one another. This cooperating group of researchers would increase its effectiveness the larger it grew and as it merged together with various other research groups. The logical limit of this merging would be a global group of researchers bound by a contract to be sincere with one another. I claim that this is exactly what we have, though the contract is not an explicit document because the researching community coalesced rather naturally and without overt ceremony. Explicit or not, the contract that binds researchers to one another is the same as the one that would bind even a small group of collaborating researchers. These, then, are the codes of academic integrity. No matter how perverted a research community may become, need would force groups of researchers to bind themselves by these codes.

The primary point is this: our codes of academic integrity are not some sort of nostalgic fantasy about a culture of honesty that managed to avoid extinction in the zoo of academia. In fact, they are absolutely necessary for getting difficult things done. Secondarily, we see that these necessary codes would have to include not only formal restrictions like agreeing to avoid plagiarism, but also a general requirement of sincerity, of aiming at getting the research right. This aim precludes lying as well as bullshit, pandering, and other failures to aim for truth.

Students are Research Initiates Who Should Accept the Necessity and Rightness of Academic Integrity Codes

Still, a student convinced that academic integrity is indispensable to research may wonder: "What does this have to do with me? Sure, if I ever become a researcher, I will play by their rules, but tonight I'm only writing a term paper! Apart from making sure I cite my sources and compose my own sentences, the codes of researchers have no relevance to my situation, right?"

There is a rebuttal to this sort of understandable skepticism, and it has to do with the fact that, regardless of his eventual intentions, by virtue of conducting research even as "practice," the student is an initiate to the community that is structured by these codes. Unfortunately, this hypothetical student can easily fail to recognize his position with respect to the community, and perhaps also the role of academic integrity in structuring that community. Bringing students to these realizations is a goal very much worth aiming at. There is great intellectual value in internalizing the full codes of academic integrity, not merely their legislated subset.

One of my teaching strategies revolves around exposing the "insane conspiracy" of high school writing teachers and telling students that I expect them to write like real researchers, that is, in the first person. In high school, students are often encouraged to avoid using the first person in their writing, presumably because it undermines the tone of "objectivity" that they are told to aim for. This is quite strange, because almost all research articles in every field (including all in my field) are written in the first person. Since the students are stating their own conclusions, I require expressions like "I think" when they write about what they think. Students often wonder why we instructors care about their opinions. In one instance, a student expressed her surprise this way: "Why do you make me write about what I think? I mean, I guess I have some opinions, but I'm not really gonna figure this out. I'm just a sophomore and philosophy isn't even my major!" This was not an attempt to dodge responsibility but a genuine question raised by a talented student who felt intimidated by my request for sincere analysis. She was comfortable with exposition, but hesitant to express her own conclusion regarding a difficult topic (whether there is a solution to Hume's problem of induction) and defend it with her best reasons. Students who feel this way must be reassured that even if they have a hard time picturing it at the moment, they will eventually have something important to say about something—and assuming that mantle in speech and writing, even in "practice" scenarios, is a way of making sure that, when that time comes, they'll know how to say it. There is a danger in this strategy, in that it may encourage bullshit: students shouldn't come away with the impression that we just want them to *act as though* they have an opinion. We should want sincerity—not pretense—and must communicate this. For this, students must be able to get A's for "I don't know" papers, in which they defend why they think there is no adequately supported conclusion regarding a certain matter.

The point is that students should eventually awaken to the realization that in their research papers, they are speaking as themselves. They should be aiming at developing and defending their views, not merely telling instructors what they want to hear. I picture this as a sort of intellectual adulthood, the stage at which the initiate inquires not only about the work of others, but also about what she thinks of that work. In doing this, she recognizes herself as a member of an inquiring community, not a mere consumer of its labors. Helping a student through this transition is perhaps the most important thing we do as educators. Once students see their writing as something said with their own voices, they realize their responsibility to say something they truly stand behind. Of course, a serious confrontation with one's own ideas and the reasons behind them is not easy. It takes courage as well as labor. The most banal way to resist this confrontation is for students literally to allow someone else's ideas to pose as their own. This is what the codes of academic integrity explicitly forbid, and such deception clearly does hinder intellectual progress.

Bullshitting, pandering, and other permitted strategies are copouts to the same extent. Successful students often rely on these strategies, and can get far without ever pausing to examine "their take" on a subject. When an instructor like me implores them to express their own views in their work, they take this as an instruction to write several paragraphs with sentences that contain the expression "I think that" while making references to the assigned texts. These sentences may be pure bullshit in Harry Frankfurt's (2005) sense—that is, statements asserted with a complete disregard for the truth (in this case, the truth of what the student really thinks about the subject, which may remain to them an unexamined matter). Nonetheless, well-written bullshit can compose a formally acceptable paper for a university course. Some such papers even earn A's, if students do a good enough job at faking genuine analysis and giving their instructor what he or she wanted to read. I am not suggesting we punish good bullshitters and panderers with bad grades. But because we care about their intellectual development, we should do our best to encourage them to reflect genuinely—to approach their subject like researchers.

Intellectual Autonomy Requires the Free Acceptance of Academic Integrity

Even though no prohibitions are violated, bullshitting and pandering (and other similar approaches) are not consistent with the full codes of academic integrity. I think this is an important point: there is more to the content of academic integrity than the rules that are listed in the university guidebooks.

Earlier, I considered a test of whether a doctor is acting as a doctor—that is, according to the foundational norms of the medical community. I distinguished between acting understandably and acting as a doctor, noting that a medical professional may do the former without doing the latter. There is a parallel for researchers: if a researcher bullshits his way through a research article, or merely mirrors the perceived prejudices of a journal's editors, he is not acting as a researcher. There is space in the research community for devil's advocates, which shows that researchers may sometimes defend conclusions they personally do not believe. However, bullshitting and (mere) pandering are clearly out of bounds. Thus, the normative bounds that constrain the activities of researchers go beyond avoiding the prohibitions against incorrect attribution, falsified data, and so forth, since bullshitting and pandering don't violate any of these explicit prohibitions. When considering the contract that would bind a small group of collaborating researchers, it is clear that bullshitting and pandering would be proscribed. Since research in general should be viewed as a global, cooperative undertaking, the same implicit contract applies.

Students should be encouraged to internalize the codes of academic integrity; these codes include all the norms that govern research, not merely the explicit prohibitions that are the focus of most discussions on academic integrity.

When I say that students should be encouraged to internalize the codes of academic integrity, I understand these codes to include all the norms that govern research, not merely the explicit prohibitions that are the focus of most discussions on academic integrity. The common thread that binds the codes into a unit is that they are the minimal norms which define the community of researchers, and thereby also their initiates, which is how I think we should see our students. This might be reason enough to encourage students, the research initiates, to adopt the codes. However, I think there is also a different and more powerful reason for this conclusion.

This reason has to do with intellectual autonomy, which requires the full codes of intellectual integrity to be internalized. Internalizing them coincides with the shift of self-perception that I described as the onset of intellectual adulthood. It is to approach the task of saying something with the same sense of responsibility that a researcher feels.

Of course, the bare request to "feel the same sense of responsibility as a researcher would" is not something that a student can simply follow. This is not to say that asking does no good, but it does need to be supplemented with reasons why he or she should feel that sense of responsibility. Those reasons, however, are familiar: they are the same reasons that require the community of researchers to abide by its own codes. The difficult thing for a student is often the realization that these same reasons *apply to her!*

Asking students to write in the first person is one aspect of my strategy to encourage this realization. Introducing the notion of peer review is another. An effective way to do this is to teach a workshop on effective peer-reviewing and then expect students to apply what they learn to improving the drafts of their peers. Students who are taught how to point out shortcomings in the work of others, especially when they know that their own work will be subjected to similar scrutiny, tend to grasp more vividly their own intellectual responsibilities. I tell them that it is their responsibility as reviewers to point out to the author that a certain point is unclear, or inadequately supported, or seems uncertain because of an unexamined objection. My students know that if they allow the mistakes of their peers to slip by them, they are failing in their task as reviewers, and this failure will be reflected in their grades. (I read, comment on, and grade all of their reviews.) This has several positive effects: one is that this activity casts students in the role of apprentice researchers, making vivid to them in a participatory way the communal aspects of research. The second positive effect is that their papers tend to be written more carefully and reflectively when they know that peers will be combing over them. A further benefit is that in following my instructions for research review, students often refine their ideas of what is and isn't adequate research.

Creative instructors can come up with many other activities in which students are treated as apprentice researchers, highlighting the continuity between them and "real" researchers. The goal is ultimately to awaken a realization that the full codes of academic integrity are necessary for research to be possible, and that every serious research endeavor presupposes the good faith and sincerity of each participant. Ironically, published policies on academic integrity may hinder the appreciation of this point, since they present integrity too narrowly. Policies tell students not to cheat, plagiarize, or falsify data. What students need to know is that we expect them to aim far higher: their aim should be to get it right. Students reach intellectual adulthood when they feel a personal obligation to get it right in their work—and when the importance of getting it right contributes to the motivation for their effort. If we contrast these motivations with those of students who aim merely at abiding by the rules and getting good grades, the difference between them is this: the former have internalized the codes of academic integrity. They grasp that these are the very glue that binds an inquiring community, and they are thinking of themselves as members of that community. They have passed the transition point at which they realize that they are responsible—and should be held responsible—for the ideas they present as their own. If this is our aim, as I think it should be, we have not adequately addressed the issue of academic integrity when we have merely explained "the rules" and found strategies to enforce them vigilantly.

Notes

1. I use this term in Harry Frankfurt's sense, in order to describe a "lack of connection to a concern for truth" and statements expressed with an "indifference to how things really are" (Frankfurt, 2005, 3-4).

2. If this argument is right, it would also justify legislating a ban on bullshit in academic work. However, I am aware of no university that forbids bullshitting, nor would I advocate such a ban. I suspect that a ban on bullshit would indeed be morally justified, though impossible to enforce without unacceptable invasions of privacy. Another possibility, however, is that a higher principle is involved: bullshitting is a "thought crime" (while deliberate falsification is something more). If institutions have no right to legislate against mere thought crimes, we have a different reason for treating these two failures of honesty so differently.

Works Cited

Akers, S. (2003). Academic integrity: A guide for students. Purdue University Office of the Dean. Available at http://www.purdue.edu/ODOS/osrr/ integrity.htm

Frankfurt, H. G. (2005). *On bullshit*. Princeton: Princeton University Press.

Syracuse University. (2006, July 1). Academic integrity policy. Available at http://supolicies.syr.edu/ethics/acad_integrity.htm

Freshman Composition as Disaster Response

James M. Pangborn

FIRST, A DISCLAIMER: this essay is meant to reflect neither well nor poorly upon the problematic disaster responses the U.S government undertook in 2005. There are political points to be made about those events, some of them quite damning, but that's none of my business here. My discussion will not issue from the politics of hegemony per se, nor from economics, but from the pragmatics of common experience, noticing first what its most expert practitioners notice: disaster response is hard—almost forbiddingly so. College writing is hard too, for many of our students, and I want to set forth what I see as a pattern of similarities between those two sets of difficulties. This is intimately relevant to our treatment of the plagiarism issue, as these difficulties might account in some measure for, among other things, students' willingness to cheat. I will develop a line of thinking initiated for me by the German psychologist Dietrich Dörner: his work *The Logic of Failure* (1997) shows how people engaged in difficult, high-stakes, time-sensitive decision making (such as disaster response, food aid planning, etc.) tend to enact a set of irrational, unwise behaviors that look a lot like the stubborn quirks of our composition students.

Let me list Dörner's most significant observations, and then I'll discuss a few of them in more detail in terms of college composition. First, he notes, people in that sort of trouble tend to neglect certain aspects of planning, especially reasonable goal setting; they tend to focus their attention with a sort of tunnel vision, leading to poor timing and a measurable neglect of side effects and practical consequences; they tend to handle the information-gathering part of their task unwisely in two complementary ways, at times getting mired in unnecessary detail and at other times ignoring obvious complicating data; they

19

tend to ascribe their problems to a single cause instead of the more usual multiplicity of causative influences; they tend to mentally leap to pseudo-problems removed vertically (that is, by increasing or decreasing abstraction) or horizontally (by association) from the problem truly at hand; they tend to revert to methods that have worked for them before, even when the earlier problems were significantly different; and they tend rather passionately to evade and reject analytical self-assessment and reflective self-regulation.

Dörner isolates and describes these tendencies by means of computer simulations—Sim City–type stuff—played by real-life disaster responders. He ramps up the pressure and complexity to approach real-world disastrousness, provoking in short order the kinds of failure he hopes to train his subjects to avoid in the long haul. My thesis is that the Dörner connection shows how high-stakes, time-sensitive fear and stress exacerbate many of the writing problems we find in college composition courses, fueling the rationalization to cheat. Luckily, Dörner's best bet to ameliorate this failure-proneness is what most of us already provide for freshman writers: lots of simulated practice with guiding feedback. But the problems are stubborn.

> *High-stakes, time-sensitive fear and stress exacerbate many of the writing problems we find in college composition courses, fueling the rationalization to cheat.*

So, which patterns of failure make the most difference in student writing? For now, three related categories will do: first, the tendency to adopt unrealistic, egocentric goals and purposes; second, tunnel vision; and third, the stubborn, almost robotic allegiance to grade-school forms and purposes that correspond, as I see it, to a kind of "knee-jerk methodism." (The residual Freudian in me wants to mention, by the way, that these are all instances of *condensation* and thus relate in some way to the trope of metonymy, the putting of the part for the whole.) Realistic, harmonious goal-setting gets frustrated in two ways, one of which hardly needs mentioning: procrastination rules! But another aspect of disturbed goal setting is more insidious: many of Dörner's overwhelmed subjects contrive to force a comforting false simplicity and clarity by focusing on foggy abstractions instead of setting pragmatic goals. Likewise, it takes a while, in my classes anyway, to persuade students that their job is more limited and practical than to prove their favorite glittering, platitudinous generality, e.g., "everyone has a right to their own opinion." In a task already fraught with pressure, Dörner's subjects and ours exacerbate their bad situations by adopting goals that are not anchored to practicality.

But consider, alongside this allegiance to high-altitude fogginess, the false clarity of grades, the number-one self-reported goal our students set for themselves. Grades are even more confoundedly confused between abstraction and concreteness than money is (see Marc Shell [1995] on money's slipperiness in this regard). They are supposed to measure "How'm I doin'," but when writing we do at least twenty things at once; the single grade represents, and thus masks, a complex multiplicity of assessment considerations. This sort of simplifycation might seem attractive as anodyne to overwhelming complexity—that is, the seeming comprehensibility of the abstract "B" understandably trumps the largely opaque complex of readers' actual reasons to feel "This paper is good, but not really outstanding." But when one's only purpose in writing is to get an "A," that purpose is practically solipsistic, and plenty of our students' papers vividly reflect this absence of actual, shareable communicative purpose.

Dörner's solution to this particular kind of failure reminds me of one of the composition teachings most resisted by my students: to include goal setting and situation assessment in a recursive routine of periodic, intermediate adjustments. Despite my describing, explaining, illustrating, and formally requiring evidence of this recursive process, I find it awfully hard to get students actually to do it, and so, I'm sure, do most of us. When the end of the semester is near at hand and yet students still ask whether they are allowed to make reasonable adjustments in the theses they had chosen before drafting (a premature choosing, contrary to my advice, of course), one gets the idea that something well beyond laziness makes them regard their initial goal choices as inviolable. Their grade-school teachers had them choose theses before drafting, and that's that. In this as in many aspects of student writing, we might be tempted to think the students simply have no common sense; but, to be fair, they might feel little reason to expect reasonableness to prevail. "Not much sense being practical," one student told me recently, "when the whole assignment seems totally impractical." Common sense, in this somewhat irrational institution, is a work in progress for us all.

On this point, let's turn to Mike Rose's idea that students often figure out their rhetorical situations in unfortunate ways. His well-known thesis in *Lives on the Boundary* (1990) is that students' writing hang-ups are not primarily emotional, as many assume. Rather, they are often what Rose calls "cognitive," meaning that they result from conscious, although mistaken, calculation. This, I think, harmonizes perfectly with Dörner's "logic of failure." Rose touches on the grade-confusion problem, for instance, in terms of those students who, Bartleby-like, prefer not to realistically assess their poor performance because they misidentify grades as markers of generalized personal worth, so when grades seem too low, they feel simply wrong, insulting, and therefore dismissible. My cross-attribution of this bad calculation to Dörner's pressure hypothesis does not contradict Rose, but rather fills out and strengthens the theory, connecting stressed-out feelings with stressed-out thought. And at the point of contact between these explanations we glimpse a very un-pretty picture of withdrawal from social interaction into an armored self. (Savvy readers will note that the residual Freudian here shows his Reichian coloration.)

Of course, high-school habits are hard to break under any circumstances, and to the extent that our students have been trained to first form a thesis and then draft a paper about it, dialogical reasoning finds no ready place in their writing routines. The set pattern of five-paragraph themes floated free from real-world purpose long ago, as a critical glance at, say, Edgar Roberts's perdurable *Writing Themes About Literature* (1991) will show. Even so, this unfortunate ground condition seems insufficient to account for the tunnel vision we encounter in students whose essays lack the give-and-take of reasonable discussion even when their classroom conversation shows them fully capable of it. My own observations on sentence-level style reinforce the Dörnerian connection: I'm thinking of those students who, however fluent in conversation, persistently write in a choppy, disconnected way, as if the act of writing narrowed their windows of consciousness to the width of only one sentence—or less, which would account for the prevalence of broken predications. Tunnel vision can help explain the uncanny recurrence of sentence-level problems such as the typical absence of—nay, resistance to—transitional phrasing and the abiding presence of sentence-structure monotony. This correlation between stress and the narrowing of attention is, by the way, a commonplace of psychology (e.g., Winstanley, 2005).

As with tunnel vision, so with knee-jerk methodism, or in our case the persistent reluctance to abandon simplistic formats and artificial, make-work purposes that are appropriate, if at all, to children's schoolwork only. Their high-pressure situation seems to dictate to risk-averse students that they must at all costs *be right*: not play, not explore, not create, but stay on safe ground. Dörner describes more than once the unfortunate twists of reasoning people under stress will perform in order to preserve their sense of their own competence, when humility would be the more realistic attitude to take. And the part of Dörner's solution appropriate to this part of the problem is very simple and yet very hard—nothing more than the oracular dictum, *gnothi seauton*, "know thyself."

"Know thyself," I want to say, is precisely what the person under high-stakes, time-sensitive pressure tends to neglect. This self-forgetting shows especially in the goal-setting arena, where Dörner's subjects tend to skip out on sustained goal assessment, leaving implicit goals opaque and conflicting goals un-reconciled. One's stress-narrowed window of attention typically leaves the self out of the critical picture. And knee-jerk methodism, when it functions as a guarantee of being right, is yet another symptom of this same forced deficit of critical self-regard. I've seen students literally drop their jaws when they realize we actually do want them to court the disaster of finding fault with their own assumptions. And egocentric defensiveness—an experiential aspect of condensation—plays prominently in all of the failings Dörner enumerates; thus our students, like his disaster responders, often stand by discredited methods, such as the template-bound high-school essay format, partly in order to ensure that failure, if it occurs, touches only the method and not the writer.

Many of these students, as my friend Tom Bertonneau pointed out to me, no matter how confused they know their writing to be, hold dear the hope that they, through the window of their compositions, will be found to be glorious after all. (I really do think they are glorious, but not in quite that way.) American exceptionalism, revved up by the opportunistic commercial media, provides a ready-made ideological support for that hope: "Hey—since there might, after all, be exceptions to any rule, I'll bet I am one!" Glitteringly reductive generalities such as "everybody's got a right to their own opinion" come to signal wishful reductions such as "every intellectual problem is a pseudo-problem if I say it is," "nobody's really an expert," and "no one can prove anything," so "anything I choose to say is inviolably personal—my opinions are sacred!" It's important to note, though, that our present, early 21st-century freshmen and sophomores grew up drinking out of milk cartons that literally advertised kidnapping hysteria in an era permeated by grievous exaggeration of the perils of life in our society. Those of us over thirty or so, I submit, have no sure way to know how that feels, but I'll bet that, in the extra-mean world this generation inhabits, exploring ideas and submitting to self-critique feels far too chancy when one can recite sparkly truisms instead—or copy and paste them off the Internet.

> *Plagiarism cannot be effectively opposed by worsening the conditions that bring it about. We may need, purposefully and publicly, to ease up on grading but buckle down on academics—get more rigorously reasonable in our expectations and our explanations.*

Intellectual maturity, as I understand it, consists in the habit of reconstructive self-examination, moderation in all things (including moderation), humility without apology, and direction not by but toward others. But the commercial wing of our culture nurtures and protects its favorite aspects of our immaturity as vigilantly as a full-blown paranoid nurtures and protects his sources of imaginary inside information. An odd thing happens, though, to those who refuse to grow up: even as they spout egalitarian platitudes, their underlying structure of assumptions tends very strongly to be authoritarian, according to which the only thing of positive value in the world of ideas is received certainty—so, at least, cognitive development theorists such as William G. Perry (1999) and Patricia King and Karen Kitchener (2004) point out. Plagiarism can thus seem a reasonable response when we demand, as I think we must, that students seriously face up to and work with uncertainty. When we present our demands in authoritarian terms, so much the worse; and when we mischaracterize plagiarism as theft or trespass, worse yet.

Plagiarism cannot be effectively opposed by worsening the conditions that bring it about. We may need, purposefully and publicly, to ease up on grading but buckle down on academics—get more rigorously reasonable in our expectations and our explanations. At present, it seems to me that learning by trial and error feels too unsafe for many of our students to willingly risk it, yet I see no other way for them to learn to write well, so something's got to give. "Maintain Standards" is an egregiously vacuous slogan unless it means standards of workmanship, honesty, usefulness, compassion, and respect. As long as students feel as though writing class is hitting them like a disaster, we should expect to receive disaster-like responses to our assignments. When we learn how to make it look and feel both fair and safe for students to accept what we offer, I believe we can cultivate genuinely purposeful thinking-through-writing with much less cheating than presently occurs.

Works Cited

Dörner, D. (1997). *The logic of failure: Recognizing and avoiding error in complex situations.* Cambridge, MA: Perseus.

King, P. M., & Kitchener, K. S. (2004). Reflective judgment: Theory and research on the development of epistemic assumptions through adulthood. *Educational Psychologist, 39*(1), 5-18.

Perry, W. G., Jr. (1999). *Forms of intellectual and ethical development in the college years: A scheme.* San Francisco: Jossey-Bass.

Reich, W. (1949). *Character analysis.* New York: Farrar, Strauss, and Giroux.

Roberts, E. V. (1991). *Writing themes about literature* (7th ed.). Englewood Cliffs, NJ: Prentice.

Rose, M. (1990). *Lives on the boundary: A moving account of the struggles and achievements of America's educationally underprepared.* New York: Penguin.

Shell, M. (1995). *Art and money.* Chicago: University of Chicago Press.

Winstanley, S. (2005). Cognitive model of patient aggression towards health care staff: The patient's perspective. *Work and Stress, 19*(4), 340-350.

Resources

Graff, G. (2003). *Clueless in academe: How schooling obscures the life of the mind.* New Haven, CT: Yale University Press.

Kegan, R. (1994). *In over our heads: The mental demands of modern life.* Cambridge, MA: Harvard University Press.

Smithson, M. (1989). *Ignorance and uncertainty: Emerging paradigms.* New York: Springer-Verlag.

Sorrentino, R., et al. (2003). The theory of uncertainty orientation: A mathematical reformulation. *Journal of Mathematical Psychology, 47,*132-149.

An Air of Integrity
Building a Preventative Classroom Environment

Amy S. Roache-Fedchenko

As TEACHING ASSISTANTS and faculty, we are often faced with countless responsibilities, and it is sometimes difficult to address issues such as academic integrity from an applied perspective. Often the policies of academic integrity are overlooked until we encounter a problem that needs immediate and direct attention. This chapter illustrates the feasibility of creating an environment that promotes academic integrity within our classrooms. Pedagogical methods and personal experiences will provide illustrations of creating a preventative classroom environment, emphasizing definitional elements of the term academic integrity.

How is Academic Integrity Defined?

To understand how to promote academic integrity, we must first understand the definition adopted by the university as a whole. Syracuse University defines academic integrity as "a commitment to the values of honesty, trustworthiness, fairness, and respect." Thus, a breach of academic integrity includes "any dishonest act which is committed in an academic context." It includes plagiarism ("the use of someone else's language, ideas, information, or original material without acknowledging the source"), copying from another student's work, use of unauthorized aids in examinations, and so forth (Syracuse University, 2007). In addition, the university and this publication, drawing from Duke University's Center for Academic Integrity,[1] recognize academic integrity as "a commitment, even in the face of adversity, to five fundamental values: honesty, trust, fairness, respect, and responsibility" (Center for Academic Integrity, n.d.).

Trust, honesty, fairness, respect, and responsibility: all vague and abstract terms that create this widely accepted definition of academic integrity. Hence, this characterization is filled with terms that, when an explanation is required, are met with a multitude of interpretations and applications. I will attempt to address the contents of these definitions in a way that promotes the applicability of these terms within the classroom.

Create a Community

The one thing that has proven to enable academic integrity on diverse campuses is the use of an honor code system or "modified" honor code system (McCabe & Treviño, 1993). Such an arrangement centers on the idea that all members of the university should be involved in the formation, maintenance, and enforcement of integrity codes. The implementation of an honor code system creates and promotes a sense of community within the diverse environment of the university, eliminating the type of "us vs. them" mentality that is often associated with institutional policy. Additionally, with this sense of cohesiveness, all members of the university share a pride and responsibility that is essential to the definition of integrity and the legacy of being part of a prominent institution, all of which have been shown to reduce cheating and plagiarism (McCabe & Pavela, 2004, 10; McCabe & Treviño, 1993, 523). This sense of community and pride is integral to the learning environment and to teachers' and students' ability to transfer integrity policies to real-life situations within the classroom.

While it is certainly not necessary that students know their peers within each course, it is conducive to a community environment. Learning the names of your students only creates half of a community, one confined to the student-teacher relationship. Informal introduc-tions or short "ice breaker" exercises related to a course theme are two ways to encourage interaction within the classroom. For instance, in teaching an anthropology course that will introduce students to the idea of culture, the ice breaker I have used requires students to think creatively in groups and interact in a way most classroom settings don't allow. In this activity, students are divided into groups and asked to create a culture with distinct forms of greetings, gender segregation, or body language. These actions created by the students communicate the

> *A sense of community and pride is integral to the learning environment and to teachers' and students' ability to transfer integrity policies to real-life situations within the classroom.*

cultural characteristics of each group, and other groups are able to observe and take note of these cultural attributes. While this may be a seemingly silly exercise, in it, students are engaged in a worthwhile activity that sets the thematic mood for the rest of the course. Students are forced to move from their comfort zone, both physically and socially, expanding their self-confidence and contributions within the micro-community of the classroom.

While an ice breaker is a good activity at the beginning of the semester, opportunities to foster relationships within the classroom should be encouraged throughout the course. Encouraging study groups and group work assignments also promote the establishment of peer-to-peer relationships, contributing to a comfortable learning environment. The idea of creating a community, or micro-community, is an integral part of the following shared experiences and suggestions for enhancing the integrity of your classroom.

Be Transparent

For establishing a comfortable learning environment, there are several characteristics students look for in an instructor. Among these are sincerity and honesty. While these terms may be abstract without a context in which to apply them, our very first encounter with our students in the classroom provides an opportunity to exhibit our candid and straightforward character. The application of these terms creates a foundation of trust and openness with our students that cultivates the learning environment throughout the semester.

During our first meeting, I often ask students to write down at least one thing they expect to gain from the class and to reflect on personal goals. In response, I listen to what students are expecting, address any concerns, and offer my own expectations of the class. I create an initial transparency of course requirements beyond those outlined in the syllabus by expressing my expectations of the students: that all students will participate in class, work hard, communicate any problems or concerns to me, and complete any assignments. This transparency places expectations out in the open for discussion and attempts to eliminate a sense of intimidation or confusion concerning what it is I expect from each person and the class as a whole. In addition, I share the expectations that I have for myself as an instructor: to provide a fair, honest, and individualized evaluation of each student. I also share a personal goal that is broadly related to class, such as guiding students to form and articulate well-informed opinions that can be expressed both verbally and in writing.

This exchange also openly identifies student and instructor responsibilities. In order to maintain a functioning community, each member must be accountable for his or her contribution, or lack thereof, to the learning environment. Through this transparent exchange of expectations and responsibilities, I begin fostering an initial culture of truth within our micro-community.

Be Truthful

Another way in which trust is established is by truthfulness. It is an incredible feeling to have a room full of students who are "clicking" with the material, readings, and discussion, fully participating and challenging themselves and others to think critically about the issues presented. As an instructor, being asked a question that you don't know the answer to can make or break the flow of interaction, and it happens to everyone at all levels of teaching. Instead of side stepping the question, avoiding the topic through a vague explanation, or formulating an answer that is beyond the subject matter (and the students' comprehension), face the question head-on as a teaching opportunity. Answer truthfully, telling the student "I don't know ... *but* we can find out and discuss this together during our next class meeting." The key to making this situation a successful learning exercise is to follow through with the last declaration. All students know when questions are being avoided, when they are being brushed off, and they can see through false knowledge. Circumvent any students' thoughts of mistrust or perception of your lack of confidence by admitting to a lapse in memory or uncertainty in providing an accurate answer.

In turn, do not dwell on a student's lack of preparedness. If a student admits to not knowing the answer to one of your questions, acknowledge his or her answer, move on, and address your concerns one-on-one with the student after class. Not only do these minute adjustments allow me to maintain authority in front of numerous individuals, but they also allow students to recognize the importance of being truthful, no matter the context or circumstances within the classroom. This technique also demonstrates your engagement and responsibility to the class. This will (hopefully) transmit to the students' own accountability within the course, reminding students that it is important to a functional class that each member within this micro-community fulfills his or her responsibilities.

Be Flexible

An apparent lack of student interest in the subject matter or disengagement with the learning environment may be an indicator of potential integrity issues. Since cheating has been shown to be correlated with disinterest, preventative action is essential in deterring indifference and cheating practices (McCabe & Pavela, 2004, 14). By attending to the classroom environment, instructors are able to preempt potential deviations from academic integrity among students. One tool for evaluating the learning processes of your "community" of students is mid-semester evaluations.

Mid-semester evaluations aid in taking preventative measures by allowing shortcomings and successes to be addressed. Each semester I give my students three open-ended response questions that ask:

1. What are the primary teaching strengths of your Instructor?

2. What are the primary weaknesses of your Instructor? Can you offer suggestions for improvement?

3. Do you feel you are receiving good instruction? Please comment on the overall quality of the section and any other issues relating to your section that you would like addressed.

This feedback allows me to improve my pedagogical style by changing techniques that students identify as needing improvement and strengthening methods that have been effective. Classrooms are composed of individuals with a variety of learning styles; changes in format, including formal and informal strategies, help to keep students engaged (Marton, Dall'Alba, & Beaty, 1993). The mid-semester evaluation helps me realize that what works for one class does not always work in another, because not all groups of students will react to or interact with the same material identically. For instance, within my Anthropology 185: Global Encounters class, mid-semester evaluations revealed that the majority of the students enjoyed the in-class discussions, but it was recommended to me that I attempt to include more in-class activities and group work. I was able to adjust to techniques that seem to best fit the flow of the class by providing students with a variety of ways to expand and express their knowledge through group or hands-on activities, open discussion, or class debates, and by modifying assessment strategies like free writing, pop quizzes, and group assignments. Through my experience, based on these adjustments, students came to class more prepared and were more interested in engaging with the course material with their peers.

Be Inspirational

Related to the previously described scenario for being truthful, promoting the importance of continual or lifetime learning is something we as members of academia greatly value. Allowing the learning environment to grow stagnant creates boredom and apathy toward the subject matter. Encouraging students to bring in outside knowledge and share personal experiences during class discussions often facilitates dialogue beyond the provided course materials or allows tangents onto related topics, both of which challenge the class to further their application of knowledge.

One way I try to promote personal development is by asking students to write their personal goals on an index card at the beginning of the course and then surveying the students at the end of the semester, enabling them to see what they have gained from the course other than knowledge of the course material. One student in my anthropology class wrote:

> As one of my first college courses, I entered the class unsure of what to expect. What I found out is that my ideas were challenged and some were changed. The topics, ethnographies and discussions forced me to think about the world in a way that is less centered around where I am, and expanded [my] views to a more macrocosmic relationship among all peoples, cultures, and customs. (student in ANT 185, Fall 2005)

Another way in which I have engaged students with course topics outside class is by providing information and material not presented within the course. As a way to create a personal connection with the class, I often include my own personal anecdotes to illustrate examples. The Internet is also a great source of real-world examples or current research on various topics. For instance, when teaching about the sociality of primates, I emailed my class a copy of a *New York Times* article about primate behavior and morality (Wade, 2007). Although this was not required reading, the article sparked interest in the topic, and a short debate ensued during the next class meeting. Furthermore, the promotion of learning as a continual process also allows us to inform students of the academic support available to them through the university, aid them in research methods and resources, and provide them with an opportunity to teach themselves.

It is our responsibility to maintain a high standard of academic integrity and to work on the transference of this ascribed ideal to practical applications within our classrooms.

Conclusion

Although the promotion of academic integrity is the central point of this publication, "teachers will find that their greatest impact on students—including inspiring a commitment to academic integrity—will come in the context of personal respect, attention, and connection" (McCabe & Pavela, 2004, 13), and it is through these character traits we as instructors will be able to foster trust, honesty, fairness, and integrity with our students.

It is our responsibility as instructors, and as current and future faculty, to partake in the integrity of the classroom and to maintain students' interest. Although time constraints, workload, and the idea of changing student behavior can be overwhelming and provide an easy excuse to be lackadaisical (McCabe & Pavela, 2004, 13-14), it is our responsibility to maintain a high standard of academic integrity and to work on the transference of this ascribed ideal to practical applications within our classrooms. In sharing my pedagogical experience, I hope I have inspired you to take the initiative to be forthright with students from the first day of class, provide an honest atmosphere within your classroom, be flexible in your pedagogical methods to enrich your micro-community, and encourage commitment to personal enrichment. By incorporating some of these strategies into our teaching philosophies, as professors, future professors, and instructors, we meet the requirement for educators to promote and maintain the academic integrity policy we have helped to create and abide by each time we gather in the classroom.

Notes

1. The Center for Academic Integrity, formerly at Duke University's Kenan Institute for Ethics, has moved during the publication of this volume. The Center is now hosted by the Rutland Institute for Ethics at Clemson University. The Center can still be found online at the same address: http://www.academicintegrity.org

Works Cited

Center for Academic Integrity. (n. d.). Rutland Institute for Ethics, Clemson University. Available at http://www.academicintegrity.org

Marton, F., Dall'Alba, G., & Beaty, E. (1993). Conceptions of learning. *International Journal of Educational Research, 19*, 277-300.

McCabe, D., & Pavela, G. (2004). Ten [updated] principles of academic integrity. *Change, 36*(3), 10-15.

McCabe, D., & Treviño, L. K. (1993). Academic dishonesty: Honor codes and other contextual influences. *The Journal of Higher Education, 64*(5), 522-538.

Syracuse University. (2007). Academic integrity policies and procedures. Available at http://academicintegrity.syr.edu.

Wade, N. (2007, March 20). Scientist finds the beginnings of morality in primate behavior. *New York Times.* Available at http://www.nytimes.com

Resources

Stearns, S. A. (2001). The student-instructor relationship's effect on academic integrity. *Ethics and Behavior, 11*(3), 275-285.

Buying A's and Counting FTEs
Plagiarism, Consumerism, and the Economics of Higher Education[1]

Michael Murphy

THERE IS—I remain convinced in my heart of hearts—a wonderfully provocative sentence somewhere in composition theorist Ann Berthoff's general oeuvre I'd like to begin here by quoting—though, since I haven't been able to locate it in my well-worn copy of the *The Making of Meaning* (1981), and all my Google searches turn up nothing, I have to acknowledge that it's possible this sentence might be part projection, the product of my sense that it's just the kind of thing the lovably cranky old Berthoff *would* say, even if she never actually has. Very roughly, then, that sentence—delivered, as my memory reconstructs it, in a talk to a room full of writing-across-the-curriculum teachers—goes something like this: "Any teacher who receives a bought paper deserves it." Always the provocateur, what Berthoff meant—and I'm sure she'd say this whether I've gotten the particulars of her sentence right or not—was that having authentic, intellectually intimate relationships with students requires a level of engagement with the work of individual students that effectively makes plagiarism impossible: get to know your students as thinkers and writers, give them assignments narrowly tied to the idiosyncratic contours of genuine class conversations, talk with them about their ideas as they develop, read their evolving drafts. *Teach* them. Then simple cheating largely disappears.

Noted plagiarism-and-authorship scholar Rebecca Moore Howard strikes similar notes in her work—particularly her shot across the bow of the profession published several years ago in the *Chronicle of Higher Education* called "Forget about Policing Plagiarism: Just *Teach*." Echoing Berthoff in noting that "We beg our students to cheat if we assign a major paper and then have no further involvement with the project until the students turn in their work" (Howard,

2001), Howard broadens Berthoff's critique (or the one I've attributed to Berthoff) to address the larger pedagogical enterprise:

> even as we're catching and punishing plagiarists in our classes, we have to ask ourselves why they are plagiarizing. Some of the possible answers to that question are not appealing.... It is possible that students are cheating because they don't value the opportunity of learning in our classes.... It is possible that our pedagogy has not adjusted to contemporary circumstances as readily as have our students. Rather than assigning tasks that have meaning, we may be assuming that students will find meaning in performing assigned tasks. (36)

Dishonesty often has something to do with disengagement, Howard suggests—and disengagement, she goes on, can have *lots* to do with bad teaching and irrelevant courses.

While I don't by any means dispute Berthoff's or Howard's sense that certain pedagogical practices help cultivate—or at least enable—student dishonesty, I'd suggest widening responsibility even a little further. Teachers work in specific moments under specific circumstances—mainly institutional ones—and to place the blame at their feet alone (which I don't believe either Howard or Berthoff means to do, actually) would be to fall prey to precisely the same sort of myopia we're so often encouraged to avoid by participants in discussions of plagiarism and intellectual property: that is, if *texts* don't begin and end with single, originary

Having authentic, intellectually intimate relationships with students requires a level of engagement with the work of individual students that effectively makes plagiarism impossible.

authors in sociohistorical vacuums, neither do courses with teachers. In fact, I'm tempted to revise the formulation I've attributed to Berthoff: "Any *university* that *needs to create a task force on bought papers* deserves them."

Of course, like Berthoff, I'm overstating for effect a bit here—but I stand by the point behind the hyperbole. To my mind, plagiarists are in large part—more than it's comfortable for many of us to acknowledge—the incorporated academy's chickens come home to roost.

It's often observed that the much-reported "rash" of plagiarism in the age of the Internet results from a specific sort of ethical problem: crass, bourgeois, Generation-AOL students' ever-increasingly "consumerist" sensibility about education. This is what Gary Pavela has described with passion and conviction as "instrumental" approaches to education. Education is something you buy, and you get what you pay for. The more expensive the paper mill, the better the product; the more prestigious the school, the better the job after graduation. The comment reportedly made by a parent calling to complain about a son or daughter's mediocre grade at the relatively expensive private university where I taught as a graduate student became notorious among colleagues as a representation of this sensibility: "But I'm not paying for C's." Obviously, it's a short slide from this idea of schooling to a bought paper, so from this perspective the problem of cheating becomes, as the title of Vibiana Bowman's (2004) opening chapter in *The Plagiarism Plague* wistfully puts it, "Teaching Intellectual Honesty in a Tragically Hip World." Student ethics seem to have disappeared somewhere in the space between the mall and the desktop.

Even someone trying as hard to understand the motivations of knowing student-plagiarists as compositionist Kelly Ritter—who feels constrained to acknowledge with sympathy "the complexity of the students' academic needs, which sometimes are in conflict with their own personal ethics and morals" (2005, 606)—imagines that the phenomenon of online paper-buying all comes back in the end to "the relationship already in place between *student* authors and consumer culture that dictates the role writing plays in one's college career" (603). While Ritter worries that we need to understand better the motivations of knowing plagiarists, whom she contends steal academic writing less because they're unethical than because they've been taught to "not believe that they can or should be authors of their own academic work" (602), she also sees students as sadly easy targets for the "consumer-driven discourse of online paper mills" (602). Our students, she laments, "frequently see college writing ... as an economic rather than an intellectual act" (603). It's for this reason, because of this commonplace association between lapsed student morality and consumer culture, that the often-repeated term recommended by Becky Howard to denounce simple dishonesty, as opposed to other inadvertent forms of plagiarism like what she calls "patchwriting," is so laden with marketplace ethics—not "cheating," she says, but "fraud." And it's for this reason, too, that Howard is so generally uncompromising, as Ritter points out, about the severity of the penalties she sees as appropriate for "fraudulent" work.

And yet, truth be told, it's difficult for me not to wonder about the degree to which higher education at the turn of the millennium, which purports to stand in horror and dismay at the proliferation of consumerist approaches to schooling, actually reinforces and perhaps even cultivates them. I find it difficult not to wonder, that is, about the degree to which we ourselves have encouraged students to see not only writing papers but going to college itself precisely as "an economic rather than an intellectual act."

I mean this not only in the sense that the general culture of higher education has, for some time now, increasingly focused on vocation and the economic promise of a college degree in its recruitment of potential students—consider most any of the TV spots for individual campuses that run endlessly during the Division I men's basketball tournament, for example—but in the sense that our managerial priorities both mark us clearly for students as a corporation and make us tangibly complicit in the circumstances surrounding the plagiarism problem. To my mind, the economic landscape of contemporary higher education, which features large lecture classes, heavy teaching loads, increasing administrative expectations, and underpaid part-time faculty teaching off the tenure track, typically makes authentic intellectual work with students—the kind of ongoing conversation between teachers and students that Berthoff and Howard have in mind (a version of the Plato-Aristotle relationship as Gary Pavela describes it)—effectively impossible. In our rush to generate FTEs[2]—the increasingly universal measure of faculty and department output calculated on the basis of total student credit hours (a language revealingly no longer reserved for academic administrators!)—we lose much of what matters most in education. I'd be lying if I said that in my own 75-seat sections of the grammar course that my institution requires of its elementary education majors I *ever* manage to work as anything like a mentor with most students, as they assemble the journals of observed nonstandard usages I assign or as they write reflections on required tutoring experiences. Even by the most conservative estimates, less than 15% of the courses taught nationally in composition and rhetoric are led by faculty on tenure lines (Coalition on the Academic Work Force, 2006)—meaning that a fair share of the 85% balance works part-time on two or more campuses. This also means that the burden of committee work, student advisement, and assessment placed in turn on the reduced core of tenure-line faculty gets ever heavier. These realities are well enough documented that I probably don't need to rehearse them further, especially to people who necessarily live with them every day. But we should keep in mind that our students live with their effects in the classroom as well—too often, big classrooms with lots of students and busy, distracted instructors—which not only makes preventative approaches to plagiarism very difficult but communicates much to students about the apparently universal urgency of bottom lines. Is it any wonder, then, if they see higher education in terms we recognize as mercenary (or "instrumental," as Professor Pavela suggests)?

To some extent, even knowledge itself is susceptible to this sort of pressure. Many have pointed out that much of the cut-and-paste dynamic is a function of a commodified notion of knowledge as content that, of course, lends itself to easy assessment (so that paper-reading becomes simply asking the question *have students reproduced the information contained in readings and lectures?*): in this model, knowledge is something to be not created by writers but gathered and collated. It's writing-as-foraging. And if knowledge is property, as students often reason, on the basis of this model, and if one has made the effort to find and assemble a coherent set of relevant passages, well then ... since possession is nine-tenths of the law, it must belong to the assembler. And of course, we can feel safe chuckling a little snidely at this sensibility—those bourgeois students again—but I've had student writers who practiced cut-and-paste plagiarism (and by that I mean assembling whole papers of nothing but gathered passages) tell me not only that they don't understand it as wrong, but that they in fact *perceived it to be the writing practice prescribed by the professors in their disciplines.*

If knowledge is property, as students often reason, and if one has made the effort to find and assemble a coherent set of relevant passages, then, since possession is nine-tenths of the law, the collection must belong to the assembler.

A magazine journalist writing about plagiarism under the pseudonym Dougie Child—herself a former writer for an online paper mill—elaborates another interesting connection between this epistemology and economics in the recent *Product Versus Process: The Term Paper Industry and the New Face of Cheating in American Education.* Child (2005) contends that an increasing preoccupation with grades and products alone in the No-Child-Left-Behind Age—not with what really happens to students intellectually, but with how many answers they get right—is responsible for encouraging students to see education in general as a matter of exchange and quantitative certification. According to Child, "The central issue" with respect to "why the term paper industry exists" is

> the priority that education places on student product. Product in this respect is the outcome of student effort: student product takes the form of grades, standardized testing, and any manner of the numerous school-related outcomes that can be interpreted as representing student academic ability. The term paper industry profits from our nation's embrace of an education system in which the product of students' efforts is perceived as more important than the process the student uses to create the product. (5)

She resolves, "Seizing [on] product-based learning as the only permissible form of education changes our views on what is acceptable in education: cheating is still wrong in principle, but it gets results" (11).

My own experiences in the classroom, for what they're worth, suggest that our students too sense an inconsistency between how we *really* function as an institution and our moral stance on plagiarism. I taught a course at SUNY Oswego called "Plagiarism, Citation, and Textual Ownership" in which we not only practice citation but also talk about it, and though I've long recognized that many students resent academic citation practices, which they see as vague, arbitrary, and even a little exclusionary (what composition teacher doesn't recognize this?), I was shocked by the stridency—and the eloquence, too—of the responses I got when I asked students early in the semester to browse some academic integrity websites. They identified what they read immediately as "a sales pitch" and even "academic evangelism." One student called an anti-plagiarism organization "a group of mercenaries brought in to fix the problems that professors don't want to," and its work seemed to strike them all as excessively punitive. Many found the language offensively "trite and cheesy," and one complained, "it reads like a civics lesson from the 1950s." You don't need to agree with these diagnoses to recognize that they have a certain real power and authenticity. Seldom have I found students more inherently invested in any topic than they seemed to be in this one, and my instincts tell me that we very much need to listen to them if we hope to have any effect on how they see this issue.

Having begun with an intentional overstatement, let me conclude more carefully, with some qualifications. I don't mean that nothing good can ever happen in lecture halls, that wise teachers can't craft plagiarism-resistant assignments for groups of 75 or 100, or—certainly—that two-campus, "freeway-flying" part-timers (who actually do so much of the teaching in our field) don't do remarkable, heroic, fascinating work with their students. (Indeed, my chair describes a system of rotating assignments, public research reports, and periodic small group meetings in his 100-seat cinema theory course that strikes me as genuinely brilliant planning—just the kind of thing really devoted and expert teachers do with difficult circumstances. And, as I've insisted in print before, much of the most innovative, sophisticated, effective teaching I've seen in composition has been done by colleagues working off the tenure track.) But I do mean that we rely far too heavily on these sorts of arrangements, that sooner or later they catch up with us, that as a rule other practices are far healthier pedagogically, that these practices send very clear signals to our students about our real values, and that until they begin to change—since under the present circumstances we have precious little hope of approximating the laudable pedagogical model of Socratic partnership I heard Gary Pavela describe—all our calls for "codes of honor" to heighten the "academic integrity" of the least powerful and well-represented among us—our students—run the risk of seeming to them a kind of empty moralizing.

Notes

1. This essay is adapted from a presentation given at the SUNY Faculty Senate Symposium on Academic Integrity in Albany, NY, in March 2006.

2. FTE="Full Time Enrollment." At many universities, Syracuse University among them, budgets are determined in part or whole by tuition, departments vie for funding competitively with other departments, and individual instructors vie competitively with other instructors within their own departments to keep teaching the courses they want; FTEs are the number of bodies in chairs, or the number of student tuitions the department our course is good for, and thus the unit of measurement by which funding and course offerings are allocated or denied. A course will be offered next term not if it's *taught well* this term but if its lecture hall is filled with tuition-paying (at full-time rates) bodies.

Works Cited

Berthoff, A. E. (1981). *The making of meaning: Metaphors, maxims, and models for writing teachers.* Upper Montclair, NJ: Boynton/Cook.

Bowman, V. (Ed.). (2004). *The plagiarism plague: A resource guide and CD-ROM tutorial for educators and librarians.* New York: Neal-Schuman.

Child, D. (2005). *Product vs. process: The term paper industry and the new face of cheating in American education.* Booklocker.com.

Coalition on the Academic Work Force. (2006). *Summary of data from surveys by the Coalition on the Academic Work Force (2004).* Available at http://www.historians.org/projects/caw/ cawreport.htm Howard, R. M. (2001, November 16). Forget about policing plagiarism: Just *teach. Chronicle of Higher Education, 48*(12), B24.Pavela, G. (2006, March). Featured lecture. In *A new look at law, policy and practice.* State University Faculty Senate Symposium, Albany, NY.

Ritter, K. (2005, June). The economics of authorship: Online paper mills, student writers, and first-year composition. *College Composition and Communication, 56*(4), 601-631.

The Science of Cheating
A Psychologist's Perspective

Benjamin J. Lovett

EVERY YEAR OR SO, another survey comes out showing that a majority of students have cheated at least once, and suddenly it seems like we have a cheating epidemic. Actually, cheating has been around at least since the first standardized exams were used to select civil servants in ancient China (Whitley & Keith-Spiegel, 2002)—even though the penalty at the time was death! Although the amount of cheating does seem to have risen in the past several decades (McCabe & Treviño, 1996), the frequent alarm calls regarding cheating do little to help us understand this behavior. More specifically, they typically fail to address the motivations behind cheating, which are our best hope at preventing it from happening at the outset. This is especially odd, given that the past decade has witnessed substantial empirical research into the topic. In this chapter, I briefly review that research, integrating research-based prevention strategies throughout.

Before I begin, two caveats. First, I'll focus on cheating that occurs in the classroom setting, almost always during a test or other evaluation. Plagiarizing term papers is a form of academic dishonesty worthy of detailed study, but it differs from classroom cheating in important ways, and we have less research to support recommendations about preventing it. Second, although understanding the motivation behind cheating requires a certain amount of empathy, readers shouldn't view the research discussed here as providing excuses for students who cheat. All moral transgressions, however severe, have causes, at least according to the perpetrators, but those causes don't excuse the behavior, nor should they necessarily affect our response to it. Our goal is to understand cheating so that we can stop it from happening, not to help us learn to tolerate it. With those thoughts in mind, let's get inside the heads of students who cheat.

One research strategy when appraising motivation for cheating is simply to ask students who admit to having cheated for their justifications. Many scholars have done just this, and we have data dating back to 1938, when high school students surveyed by W. W. Ludeman described the pressure to get good grades as its primary motivating factor. Many more recent studies have been conducted, and the same few reasons tend to recur in students' responses: (a) competition for good grades, (b) inadequate time to study for exams, (c) unfair or overly difficult assignments, and (d) a lack of interest in the course and material (Cizek, 1999).

Admittedly, these reasons may be rationalizations used by cheaters to assuage their guilty consciences, but if we can keep students from using those rationalizations, they may be kept from cheating in the first place. There are, then, two practical implications of these commonly offered reasons. First, instructors should take pains to present their assignments as fair and meaningful tasks organized into a workload that is reasonable, at least by the official standards of the academic institution (for example, 3 hours of work for each credit). When discussing reading assignments on the first day of class, instructors should discuss how they decided how much reading to assign and how much time students should expect to devote to the reading. Second, instructors who grade using a curve should know that it may exacerbate the sense of competition between students. Specifically, if your class's grading system is set up in such a way that only a certain percentage of students will receive A's or B's, students know that they are being judged against each other, rather than against a common standard, giving them another reason to cheat.

All of this is based on students' self-reported justifications for cheating, which have obvious limitations, especially when used as the sole method of investigation. Rather than directly asking students about their reasons for cheating, some researchers have instead examined the correlations between cheating behavior and other student characteristics. In these studies, there is no experimental manipulation; students are asked to complete a brief survey reporting their own cheating behavior as well as one or more other measures (for example, a demographic questionnaire or personality test). Cizek (1999) and Whitley (1998) each conducted a comprehensive review of the correlates of cheating, and their reviews agree on many points. Both found the following demographic factors to be associated with a higher (statistical) risk of cheating: being male, holding down a full-time job, and belonging to a fraternity or sorority. The relationship between age, year in school, and cheating is more complex; more upperclassmen than freshmen cheat, but if year in school is held constant (e.g., when considering only sophomores), older students in that year are less likely to cheat than younger students are.

What can we take from these correlations? Obviously, we should not use demographic variables to suspect students of cheating or to relieve them of suspicion. However, we can use these statistics in two ways. First, when discussing issues of academic integrity with the class as a whole, statements can be targeted to upperclassmen ("Many of you are getting close to graduating ...") or other high-risk groups. Second, these statistics lead to possible explanations of elevated cheating rates. In particular,

Making test-preparation activities part of students' grades may help them prioritize studying among their other commitments.

students who have additional responsibilities (e.g., employment) or time-consuming commitments (e.g., fraternity activities) may be less willing to devote time to studying for tests, leading to more cheating. If this is indeed the case, making test-preparation activities part of students' grades (e.g., handing in answers to review questions) or part of class itself (e.g., brief review sessions) may help. Speaking to the concerns that underlie this lack of preparation ("I know that many of you have a busy week ahead ...") can also help to address and modify students' choices when setting priorities, keeping students from rationalizing that, since their instructor doesn't understand their situation, they're justified in breaking the rules that the instructor sets.

Psychological traits are somewhat stronger correlates of cheating than demographic factors are; three such traits have shown the most consistent associations (Cizek, 1999). First, there is a particularly robust relationship between a "grading" motivational orientation and cheating: students who are motivated by grades rather than a desire to understand the material are far more likely to cheat. Second, students who feel alienated or dissatisfied with school life are more likely to cheat. Finally, higher levels of anxiety about academic performance put students at risk for cheating. These three variables may all lead to cheating via a common pathway. They all lead students to care less about the real goal of classes: mastery of knowledge and skills.

If the relationship between caring about learning and cheating is causal in nature—that is, if students with mastery goals cheat less *because* of their goals, one question comes to mind: can we change students' goals and motivational orientations? Ormrod (2003) reviewed evidence suggesting that we can, and she gives several strategies for doing so. These include pointing out the real-world utility of knowledge and skills covered in class, emphasizing the importance of deep understanding rather than rote memorization, and encouraging students to view instructors as resources for learning rather than just as lecturers and exam graders.

So far, the research reviewed and strategies proffered in this chapter have focused on making cheating "unnecessary" by providing students with strategies for academic success. As helpful as many of these strategies are, some students will inevitably elect to cheat anyway. Thus, we must also motivate students not to cheat by providing negative consequences for cheaters, attending to the "cost" side of the cost-benefit calculations that students engage in, at least implicitly, when deciding to cheat. Indeed, in the sophisticated models of cheating behavior developed by Whitley (1998) and Murdock and Anderman (2006), students' perceptions of their ability to cheat, their risk of getting caught, and the likely consequences of being caught all play major roles as disincentives to cheating.

Students who feel alienated or dissatisfied with school life are more likely to cheat.

Three suggestions follow naturally from this "economic" model of cheating. First, instructors should make the costs of cheating explicit and obvious to students. On the first day of class, as well as on test days, students should be reminded that cheating will not be tolerated and that punishment will be certain. I often tell students that I will take all actions that are available to me as an instructor; this is a bit vague, but it lets students know that I will pursue cases of cheating passionately. Second, instructors should make cheating easy to detect by arranging the students' seats so that students are not too close together and so that an instructor has room to walk in between seats to get a closer look at students, if necessary. The idea here is to keep students from even considering cheating by making it not worth the risk. Third, instructors shouldn't stay at the front of the room for the entire testing time, but should instead walk around the room, perhaps in between rows of seats; this gives students an opportunity to ask clarification questions as well as letting students know that the instructor takes proctoring seriously. I usually walk around every 15 minutes during an exam, with a constant look of interest (raised eyebrows and a half-smile) on my face, to let students know that I'm not walking over to their chair to accuse them of cheating, but just to check on how the test is going.

Some colleagues whom I respect as teachers have vehemently disagreed with me about these strategies, as well as those discussed earlier. Our job as instructors, they say, is not to motivate students not to cheat, but to teach content and skills, and if students *do* cheat, they get punished anyway, so why spend time persuading them not to cheat? No doubt some readers of this chapter will agree, and so I want to take this opportunity to answer that criticism. Simply put, a cheating-related confrontation between a student and an instructor never ends well. If the student admits to cheating, the instructor is faced with the difficult task of determining and applying appropriate consequences, and if, as is often the case, the student denies having cheated, the instructor is in an even worse position. Either way, if the instructor penalizes a student, the student may appeal, sometimes turning the event into a "he said, she said" affair. As an instructor, I'll do almost anything to avoid this situation, but I only see one reasonable, ethical way of doing so: making sure that students don't cheat in the first place. When considering the increasingly complex procedures for handling academic dishonesty at the college level, you can't help but realize that an ounce of prevention is worth a pound of cure.

All this means that I don't bring books to read while my students are taking an exam, and that I have to carefully prepare a few comments about cheating to be delivered on each exam day. It means that I spend time thinking about how to present my course assignments so that students will be persuaded to study for exams and won't feel the need to cheat. Occasionally, it can be inconvenient, but this extra effort keeps me from dealing with academic integrity disputes, from awkward meetings with department chairs and student conduct committees, and from adversarial e-mail exchanges with accused students whose honesty I usually can't determine with much confidence. This frees me up so that I can focus on designing engaging lectures, relevant class activities, and valid evaluation procedures—in short, it lets me focus on teaching. I can't agree more with my colleagues that we're here, first and foremost, to teach, not to police student conduct. But it's by thoughtfully doing the latter that I can spend less time in the academic integrity office and more time where I'm needed—in the classroom, with my students.

Works Cited

Cizek, G. J. (1999). *Cheating on tests: How to do it, detect it, and prevent it.* Mahwah, NJ: Erlbaum.

Ludeman, W. W. (1938). A study of cheating in public schools. *American School Board Journal, 96,* 45.

McCabe, D. L., & Treviño, L. K. (1996, January/February). What we know about cheating in college: Longitudinal trends and recent developments. *Change, 28*(1), 29-33.

Murdock, T. B., & Anderman, E. M. (2006). Motivational perspectives on student cheating: Toward an integrated model of academic dishonesty. *Educational Psychologist, 41,* 129-145.

Ormrod, J. E. (2003). *Educational psychology: Developing learners* (4th ed.). Upper Saddle River, NJ: Merill.

Whitley, B. E., Jr. (1998). Factors associated with cheating among college students: A review. *Research in Higher Education, 39,* 235-274.

Whitley, B. E., Jr., & Keith-Spiegel, P. (2002). *Academic dishonesty: An educator's guide.* Mahwah, NJ: Erlbaum.

Atheists and Evangelical Zeal
The Dilemma of Plagiarism and Originality

Matthew Bertram

PLAGIARISM IS WRONG. I know this because I am told as much. I cannot read a course syllabus without encountering a university-mandated section on the evils of plagiarism. But I ask, somewhat in the guise of a devil's advocate, what if plagiarism isn't as bad as we think? What if plagiarism is not paramount among scholarly sins? I know these questions may sound almost blasphemous to the academically minded. But they are the focus of this discussion.

Many cling to negative notions about plagiarism and textual ownership with almost religious conviction. Their bible is Originality. They are its disciples. Some even speak of plagiarism with the fervent delivery of a televangelist. Take, for example, Dr. Morris Freedman, currently a professor at the University of Maryland. He wrote an essay entitled "The Persistence of Plagiarism, the Riddle of Originality" for the *Virginia Quarterly Review* in 1994. In his essay he states:

> The plagiarist pollutes the universe of achievement. He wants us to give his stolen object our stamp, our respect as his property. At best he makes an alloy of what should be pristine. At worst he soils, despoils, the idea of original creation. He is worse than the censor, who, in killing a book, Milton said, kills reason itself. The plagiarist kills a man's soul, denying him recognition of his self, his offspring. He mocks originality, destroys distinctiveness, blasphemes against creation.

While I respect his passion, I find it difficult to be converted to his degree of intensity on the subject from this preaching alone. The *Areopagitica* (Milton's famous pamphlet wherein Dr. Freedman found his quote) was meant as a testament to free speech and against censorship imposed by Parliament. I will draw on this little piece of information again. On researching Dr. Freedman's background, I discovered that, as one might guess from the quote, one of his academic focuses is John Milton and seventeenth-century literature. This is intriguing on a couple of levels.

First, it could explain his almost religious conviction on the subject of textual originality. Milton's life and works were heavily influenced by his own religious beliefs. It would be reasonable to assume that one of his scholars would embody the same degree of passion on any number of subjects, including non-religious ones. Secondly, I wish to briefly examine an instance from Milton's history that may cast Dr. Freedman's argument in a slightly different light.

As Alexander Lindey points out in his book *Plagiarism and Originality*, in a study of *Paradise Lost* "Voltaire found that Milton had reproduced more than two hundred verses from [Masenius's] *Sarcotis*" (1952, 77). Now, this does not necessarily reflect negatively on Milton's work. He was writing at a time when textual originality was not as strict a discipline as it is today. Many of our greatest writers borrowed from other sources. But with even this single instance in mind, one must inevitably wonder how a man such as Dr. Freedman (and by this I mean someone so academically praised and accomplished) can be so devoted to a literary "borrower" and still be so passionate against plagiarism. We must then also question Dr. Freedman's use of Milton's own words to further his crusade against plagiarism, when it seems Milton himself was guilty of this sin, at least in the case of Dr. Freedman's apparent definition of the subject. It even seems likely that Milton himself would not have been opposed to the idea of borrowing, and may have even been advocating its practice as a form of free speech (in terms of the historical timeframe, of course) in his *Aeropagitica*.

But for the moment, let us put plagiarism in a more academic light. Rebecca Moore Howard talks about the notion of authorship and textual ownership in her essay "Plagiarisms, Authorships, and the Academic Death Penalty." In one section, she talks about the lack of the idea of plagiarism in the premodern era. She quotes Giles Constable: "The term plagiarism should indeed probably be dropped in reference to the Middle Ages, since it expresses a concept of literary individualism and property that is distinctly modern" (Howard 1995, 789). So we have only relatively recently become so preoccupied with the notion of originality in text.

So where was the notion of textual ownership, as it is defined today, during and before the Middle Ages? As Constable states, it didn't really exist. But that is not to say the past did not have its own views on the subject. "Sixteenth-century English writers before the accession of Elizabeth practiced the classical theory of imitation quite as consistently as their contemporaries on the continent, but discussed it infrequently" (White, 1965, 38). The way that Harold Ogden White describes it sounds eerily similar to some aspects of religion during the

Renaissance. Instances of prostitution and other immoral actions were accepted almost silently by the church. St. Thomas Aquinas once said: "Prostitution in the towns is like the cesspool in the palace; take away the cesspool and the palace will become an unclean and evil-smelling place." Queen Mary I herself was opposed to the infamous Bridewell prison, allegedly fearing that the great number of prostitutes held there would leak information about England's religious leaders' sexual adventures.

Somewhat in the same vein, we have issues of textual ownership. Borrowing was accepted and even praised in some cases, even though it was not precisely an act of originality. An excellent example of this is the play *Troilus and Cressida* by William Shakespeare. Before Shakespeare it was *Troilus and Criseyde*, written by Geoffrey Chaucer. Chaucer copied the story from Boccaccio's *Il Filostrato*. Boccaccio took the tale from Benoit de Sainte-Maure's *Roman de Troie*. Time and again this tale has been adopted by a disciple of literature and molded to fit his or her desires.

This steady progression of borrowing one story and slightly revising it to fit the writer's style was commonplace. But it was almost never an act of disrespect towards the author or the text (except perhaps in claims that the new version was superior to the original). Herein lies the "atheist" view of plagiarism. These authors did not believe in any "god" of pure originality that was to be both worshipped and feared. Borrowing for them was neither wrong nor indicative of an injustice. Imitation was the finest form of flattery, as it were. "Commend me to a pilferer," Byron has said; "you may laugh at it as a paradox, but I assure you the most original writers are the greatest thieves." While Byron may have called the borrower a "thief," he was clearly not using the term disparagingly, and may even have meant it as praise. To Byron, what we see as originality are simply the cleverest instances of hiding what the author has "stolen." His statement could be a reference to a Shakespeare or a Chaucer, whose works are regarded by many as cornerstones of literature but are often imitations of other works.

So here is our paradox: how can we, as academics and worshippers of the written word, enforce plagiarism as an iron law but simultaneously praise the many "borrowers" as men and women of genius and timeless literary scope? How can we be proponents of originality when the notion itself is so loosely attached to the literary canon? The answer, I believe, lies not in a strict definition of originality, but in a slightly different application of it.

This may be a slightly cynical viewpoint, but for me, it is hard to comprehend the possibility that originality is not dead. At this point, there are roughly six billion minds on this planet that have active thought processes every day. Mathematically, that is roughly 2,190,000,000,000 thought processes per year, even if we give people credit for only a single thought daily. Nor does it take into consideration all of the people who have passed on since the dawn of conscious thought. Now try to fathom the possibility that when you have a single thought, someone else has not had the same one before. It seems a bit daunting to me when it is looked at statistically.

So if we assume my argument that any single, original thought is logically almost impossible, we can gain a kind of deliverance from the chaos in the notions of imagination. Anne Berthoff (1981) offers this hope: "If we can reclaim imagination as a speculative instrument, there's a good chance we can think our way through and beyond the misconceptions of language and learning that currently abound" (33). We can work toward Paulo Freire's notion of a "pedagogy of knowing," which Berthoff describes as "a method of teaching that recognizes the human need and ability to shape, discriminate, select: the mind's power to form" (33). "Form" and "shape," in terms of the imagination, can give new hope to the idea of originality.

I do believe that plagiarism is wrong. But that does not mean it isn't a problematic topic. There is a difference, in my mind, between copying a pre-existing work out of laziness or wicked intent and imitating an influential work or style out of respect for the original. However, universities do not usually make that distinction when dealing with textual originality. If I decided to rewrite Milton's *Paradise Lost* with the desire to contemporize it to appeal to my generation, but still borrowed hundreds of lines from the original, I would certainly be in as much trouble academically as if I printed out an essay online because I didn't feel like writing one myself.

The more we establish plagiarism as an evil and blasphemous weapon against originality, the more we put fear into our students. This approach can be almost puritanical. Candace Spiegelman (1998) conducted a study on peer review and published her findings in an essay titled "Habits of Mind: Historical Configurations of Textual Ownership in Peer Writing Groups." In her work, she observed that students shied away from using useful comments during peer editing because they felt the piece would no longer be "their own." They feared a loss of textual ownership, even at the expense of what could be a more concise, coherent piece of writing. I do not believe that this should be the case. It shows a literarily crippling fear in terms of students' perceived originality and textual ownership.

Another academic gray area that we hear horror stories about, and that I want to briefly consider, is that of improper citations. At what point do we deem that the student has fallen out of the realm of ignorance into that of intent? Undoubtedly, ignorance of proper form is an issue that needs to be addressed with any student where it becomes evident. But, in my mind at least, it shouldn't warrant the failure of a class or expulsion from a school. The student should not be cast out like a leper when all that is needed is a little help and compassion for his or her situation.

The notion of true textual originality has become reminiscent of a religion. We fear it as much as we praise it. We claim to see its imprint all around us, but we have difficulty presenting concrete examples. And not everyone believes in the same ideals when originality is involved. Schools of thought on the subject can be as different as Christianity is to Buddhism or Hinduism is to Judaism.

Textual ownership and originality present a dilemma. It would be nearly impossible to find common ground between the "atheists" that praise the achievements of the borrower culture and the "evangelicals" that preach the righteousness of originality and the blasphemous evils of plagiarism. Lindey (1952) says it well when he states:

> Three things should be said at the outset. First, there is no such thing as absolute, quintessential originality. Second, plagiarism and originality are not polar opposites, but the obverse and reverse of the same medal. Third, originality—as commonly understood—is not necessarily the hallmark of talent or the badge of genius. (14)

To assume that plagiarism is as simple as the paragraph placed on a syllabus saying "don't" is folly. To understand that it is a malleable and fluid subject is the doorway to a new understanding. In the end, I would like to believe that academia's definition of "true" originality is not as important to the academic world as imagination. Searching for that form of originality is intrinsically futile, whereas searching for a unique imagination is an ultimately noble cause. This is not to say that the rules on plagiarism should be rewritten in academia, but that its pedagogy should be re-envisioned. The concrete, black and white rules at colleges and universities do not suit the flexible nature of textual borrowing. I am a devout follower of Berthoff's claims that academia could use more imagination, in both the student and faculty populations. But the real question is: what do you believe?

Works Cited

Berthoff, A. (1981). *The making of meaning: Metaphors, models, and maxims for writing teachers*. Portsmouth: Boynton/Cook.

Freedman, M. (1994, Summer). The persistence of plagiarism, the riddle of originality. *Virginia Quarterly Review*. Available at http://www.vqronline.org/articles/1994/summer/freedman-persistence

Howard, R. M. (1995, November). Plagiarisms, authorships, and the academic death penalty. *College English, 57*(7), 788-806.

Lindey, A. (1952). *Plagiarism and originality*. Westport, CT: Greenwood.

Spiegelman, C. (1998). Habits of mind: Historical configurations of textual ownership in peer writing groups. *College Composition and Communication, 49* (2), 234-255.

White, H. O. (1965). *Plagiarism and imitation during the English Renaissance*. New York: Octagon.

II

GRADUATE STUDENTS AS STUDENTS

GRADUATE STUDENTS occupy the middle position of the large university equation: faculty and students both, they are also neither *fully*. This academic double identity comes with gifts, but more often the overly conscientious graduate student feels both mostly as an extra burden. Graduate student life is perhaps all the work of being a student and most of the responsibility of being a faculty member. Because graduate students have demonstrated themselves proficient enough to earn a place in a competitive program, they assume that they need to show themselves as expert everywhere possible. Graduate students, encouraged to show competency consistently in class, get nervous about showing any weakness at all. Ironically, this dynamic operates most fiercely at the beginning of the graduate student's career—when he or she knows the least.

This presents several problems on the level of academic integrity. The most obvious of these, familiar from the undergraduate context, are the neglect of source citation and misrepresenting another's work as one's own. But these infractions may be inadvertent. Choosing a discipline means being disciplined into a particular kind of research. These scholarly habits may be assumed. The silence around the discipline's operational ideology is often not broken until an untutored graduate student stumbles because of some misstep. Who is accountable?

Another area of academic integrity relates to the mentoring process. Whether it be administrative details like deadlines or larger concerns like research opportunities, most graduate students get tangled in one or another arcane web of policy. Graduate students learn the proverbial "hard way." However, due to competitiveness for jobs and coveted positions, grads may or may not pass their hard-earned wisdom along willingly, creating a gray area of integrity in the graduate student community. How much of a "good neighbor" are graduate students to one another, inducting others into the special knowledges that are undocumented or poorly documented and circulated erratically?

Authors in this section take up these and other issues. David Nentwick addresses the dynamic of integrity around graduate student writing. In seeking help and getting oriented to a discipline-specific style of writing, how can teachers, students, mentors, and writing instructors keep others accountable for making one's original work one's own when one is simultaneously a neophyte? His conclusions will be relevant for anyone who has ever found him- or herself stuck with too many footnotes and nothing to say. Ryan Thibodeau provides readers with a wealth of experience and examples of how mentoring relationships can be established, preserved, and restored. As professionals who are prized for both their independent thinking and faithful following, graduate students living this double identity will find good mentoring in the following chapters.

Ethical Issues in Graduate Writing

David Nentwick

THE ISSUE OF ACADEMIC integrity and student writing has taken on a particular urgency in the age of the Internet and Turnitin.com. The stakes are highest in graduate education, where the emphasis is on the production of individual and original research. Graduate-level writing demands that students negotiate a variety of unfamiliar genres, learn new disciplinary vocabularies and stylistic conventions, and establish complex relations with previously published disciplinary scholarship. In the most fundamental way, scholarship *is* writing, and the process of becoming an advanced-level academic writer is simultaneously an acculturation into the discourse community of the academy and part of a student's professional development. However, writing instruction at the graduate level is not often formalized in any sort of structured and directed way, and many graduate students must build and rely upon a support network of instructors, colleagues, writing tutors, and editors to help them meet these challenges successfully. In this essay I draw on the contemporary scholarship of writing specialists dealing with plagiarism, academic integrity, and graduate student writing to identify and examine issues of academic integrity that arise when graduate students get help with their writing. This chapter focuses on the importance of establishing and maintaining ethical relationships among teachers, students, and writing consultants in order to develop the atmosphere of collegiality necessary to teaching the practices of academic integrity to future scholars and teachers. First, I attempt to give readers a feel for the contemporary climate in academia by presenting tales from the field: real-life stories that reflect current trends in thinking about writing and academic integrity. I then go on to show how these trends are codified in the language of plagiarism policy and argue that these trends have resulted in the establishment of an unhealthy—perhaps even harmful—ethics of graduate student writing. I argue that these ethics can be traced back to myths about writing, originality, and collaboration that have gained currency in academia, and I conclude by suggesting that teachers, students, and administrators alike are responsible for creating an alternative, more positive ethics of graduate writing.

"Plagiarism" and Academic Integrity

Graduate research and scholarship are typically presented in writing: in seminar papers, research reports, conference presentations, and published articles. While graduate-level research presents the opportunity for academic dishonesty, instances of such offenses as those listed on the Syracuse University Academic Integrity Office website under sections IIB and IID of the university Policy[1] are likely to be rare. Most often, the terms "cheating" and "academic dishonesty" are used when talking about plagiarism. Indeed, it is the potential for plagiarism that is greatest, since plagiarism is first and foremost an issue that arises from presenting research in written form, and writing is the primary, if not the only, medium in which research is presented. There are indeed some unscrupulous researchers out there, willing to falsify or manipulate data or break confidentiality and steal the work of others in order to pursue their own selfish goals. Unfortunately, the doors to research and scholarship that have been opened by the digital, computerized world of the Internet and word processing also lead to increased opportunities for the appropriation of others' words and ideas, to the current jeremiad against cheating, and to the development of plagiarism detection software. More often than not, it is not appropriation itself that constitutes a violation of academic integrity; rather, it is unauthorized or unacceptable appropriation that leads to accusations of academic dishonesty.

The Syracuse University Office of Academic Integrity has adopted language from the Council of Writing Program Administrators' position statement on plagiarism ("Defining and Avoiding Plagiarism: WPA Statement on Best Policies") to define plagiarism as follows: "In an instructional setting, plagiarism occurs when a writer deliberately uses someone else's language, ideas, or other original (not common-knowledge) material without acknowledging its source" (Council of Writing Program Administrators, 2003). Graduate student writing presents particular concerns to those who genuinely wish to promote an atmosphere of honesty, trust, fairness, respect, and responsibility among the graduate community and across the entire campus. At this advanced level of study, teachers tend to expect that graduate students are familiar with and well versed in the writing tasks they are asked to complete. However, many teachers do not have the time, the disposition, or the teaching tools required to offer the kind of writing instruction that many graduate students need to be successful scholars. Thus graduate students are challenged to seek out and find the writing support they need.

Tales from the Field

Because many graduate students seek help with their writing, and because they are expected to produce original work, the problem of engaging in "unauthorized cooperation in completing assignments" (Syracuse University, 2005) takes on special urgency for faculty, students, and administrators, even more so given the current rhetoric of "crisis" that prevails in contemporary public debates about academic integrity. I offer two brief anecdotes from my own experience as someone who regularly works with graduate student writers in illustration of two particular aspects of this "crisis."

Anecdote #1. In August of 2006, during the orientation for new graduate students at Syracuse University, I approached a representative of the Graduate School and asked if I could leave promotional flyers for the newly created Graduate Editing Center (GEC). I was asked a question or two about the GEC and then the conversation turned very serious, as I was advised to see to it that the GEC would run every piece of student writing it received through some kind of plagiarism detection software or service. I was informed that graduate students (in the sciences, especially) were cheating at epidemic levels, and that the GEC should be the "front line" in the fight against academic dishonesty. In short, regardless of the intentions of the GEC's creators and editors, this stakeholder in graduate student education felt that GEC editors should place policing, rather than teaching, at the top of their priority list.

Anecdote #2. Several months later, near the end of the Fall 2006 semester, a Ph.D. student and teaching assistant in geography adamantly and somewhat resentfully demanded to know why the instructors of the university's writing courses had not done something to take care of the plagiarism problem. This TA was frustrated by the dishonest behavior of his students and at a loss regarding what action ought to be taken in response. In the mind of this teaching assistant, the task at hand was to teach students the content of the course. Issues related to writing, such as plagiarism, were somehow not related to content and were, therefore, the responsibility of somebody else.

Brief as they are, these anecdotes highlight a number of remarkable perceptions about the "crisis" of academic integrity: 1) issues of academic integrity and plagiarism are frequently blurred together, so that in everyday terms they become one and the same thing; 2) graduate student cheating is an epidemic; 3) forensic technology should be employed to combat these offenders and bring them to justice; 4) teachers might not be adequately prepared to handle cases of suspected academic dishonesty; and, most significant, 5) the responsibility for addressing issues of academic integrity and the prevention of plagiarism resides solely with writing instructors and consultants.

A Police State?

The current state of affairs illustrated by these examples is, at best, unhealthy and, at worst, damaging to efforts to establish a culture of academic integrity. However, we should not be surprised, since much of the language found in academic integrity statements and policies reinforces the notion that we are in a state of moral crisis. The definition of academic integrity included in the invitation to contribute to the present volume reads as follows: "Duke University's Center for Academic Integrity defines academic integrity as 'a commitment, even in the face of adversity, to five fundamental values: honesty, trust, fairness, respect, and responsibility.'" The experts at Duke[2] suggest that it will require some sort of heroic and noble effort to act honestly, responsibly, and fairly and to give and receive trust and respect in the current "adverse" climate where cheating is the norm.

The information publicly available on the Syracuse University Office of Academic Integrity website is similar. While "educational strategies" are listed among the procedures for preventing behavior that might be construed as dishonest, a closer look reveals that these strategies have not been developed or implemented to nearly the same extent as the procedures and policies for policing and punishing suspected dishonesty. And Syracuse University is not alone; most such statements of policy and procedure imply a discipline-and-punish model grounded in a commitment to uncovering and dealing with dishonest behavior that "interferes with moral and intellectual development, and poisons the atmosphere of open and trusting intellectual discourse" (Syracuse University, 2005).

As a result of the overemphasis on detecting, policing, and adjudicating, the call for a commitment to laudable values such as the one quoted above from the Duke University Center for Academic Integrity becomes more a call to join the police force than an attempt to raise consciousness about issues of academic integrity and to establish ethical, collegial relationships between teachers and students.

Myths About Writing, Originality, and Collaboration

As graduate student writers and teachers, how do we navigate the potentially dangerous waters that lie between "unauthorized" and "authorized" cooperation? Questions about what constitutes "authorized" and "unauthorized" cooperation in graduate-level writing arise from unrealistic and outdated notions about the "individuality" and "originality" of researched writing and about writing in general. For example, consider the following:

1. If a graduate student is working on an article for publication or a dissertation chapter, and receives directions from a professional writing consultant or from a roommate on how to better organize an argument or craft a more persuasive presentation of data, is that student stepping over the line?

2. If a graduate student submits a paper to an editor or peer reviewer so that his or her written English more closely approaches Edited American English (EAE), is that student stepping over the line?

One unrealistic and outdated notion underlying these questions is: writing = thinking. Often, this assumption materializes during assessment: faulty writing = faulty thinking. As the historic body of literature on human thought and the growing body of literature on the complexities of writing and writing instruction have shown, we are far from understanding the nature of either enterprise—let alone the relationship between the two. The fear is that if someone shows us how to present our argument better, then it just may be that someone else has done not only our writing for us, but has also done our thinking for us and has thereby rendered the knowledge/product "unoriginal." However, those of us who have struggled to find the best way to communicate what we know to others (in other words, all of us)

> *Questions about what constitutes "authorized" and "unauthorized" cooperation in graduate-level writing arise from unrealistic and outdated notions about the "individuality" and "originality" of researched writing and about writing in general.*

understand that writing is an act of communication that aims at getting a *representation* of what we know into words on paper, and often times we miss the mark the first time around. A poorly organized text is not necessarily a window onto a poorly organized brain. By the same token, a revised draft that better presents an author's ideas does not prove that, somehow, the author has miraculously become "a better thinker." When we think about the relationship between writing, revision, and collaboration with a colleague or instructor, it is important to remember that working collaboratively to construct a better representation of a graduate student's knowledge does not amount to tampering with that student's data, interpretations, or conclusions, or with how that student situates his or her work in relation to other scholars in the field. It may simply mean that the writing has improved.

Another myth that gives rise to concerns about "unauthorized cooperation" takes the demand for originality in research a step further: writing is a solitary act. Our cultural imagination is filled with images of the lone, struggling, misunderstood artist burning the midnight oil and waiting for inspiration from the muse to make it possible for just the right words to be written on the page. Further underlying this myth is the American tradition of "rugged individuality," the modern day version of which is "do it yourself!" Thus, as graduate student researchers, we must somehow find unclaimed territory on which to stake an intellectual claim and then mine that claim with our own bare hands if we expect to reap the rewards.

Of course, researchers will never be able to find this unclaimed territory without the exploration and mapping that has been done by previous researchers. After all, how does one discover a gap in the research without first coming upon a body of established work? As researchers and writers, we work, as Rebecca Moore Howard (1999) would say, "in the shadow of giants." We build on what is already there; we work alongside the already existing research to situate our own work in relation to what has come before. Moreover, there is not a single word of published research that does not come under the knife of the editor's blue pencil. Nobody believes that Einstein's editors tainted the originality of his work, but everyone is glad they made his research easier to read. And if Albert shared his work in progress with a friend who helped him better match his verb forms with the subjects of his sentences, no one would consider that writing to be someone else's. A good editor, mentor, or reviewer provides help and advice, but does not do the writer's work for him or her.

Whose Responsibility?

Contemporary research in writing assessment explodes the myth that quality of thinking and originality of work can be determined in a transparent way through assessment of a written product, and it provides a framework for a complex understanding of writing. As Roberta Camp reminds us,

> Writing [is] a rich, multifaceted, meaning-making activity that occurs over time and in a social context, an activity that varies with purpose, situation, and audience and is improved by reflection on the written product and on the strategies used to create it. This understanding ... is not well served by our traditional [assessment] formats (1996, 135).

If writing is a social activity, something done in relation with others, and if writing is improved through processes of revisiting, revising, and reflection, then who decides which others we are authorized to cooperate with, and who decides what kinds of cooperation are acceptable?

The responsibility for making these determinations lies with teachers, as is clearly indicated in the Syracuse University Academic Integrity Office's educational strategies, which state that Syracuse University instructors (professors, instructors, lecturers, and teaching assistants alike) will:

> f. Implement pedagogical strategies for creating an environment that promotes academic honesty and have access to resources for necessary assistance
> g. Direct students to resources for assistance in ensuring academic honesty in their writing and researching. (Syracuse University, 2005)

Teachers must remember that their teaching is much more than the delivery of course content. Especially for graduate students, who are tomorrow's professors-in-training, the educational experience is a process of acculturation into the conventions of knowledge production within and outside the academy. Much of this acculturation work happens during the writing process, beginning with a student's introduction to research practices and continuing through such writing assignments as summary and synthesis of required readings, seminar papers, qualifying examinations, dissertation proposals, and theses and dissertations. Each of these written products comes with a set of conventions that frame the relationship between the writer, her knowledge, and disciplinary knowledge, all of which ultimately shape the written product itself. Producing written products, then, is practically equivalent with "scholarship." Quite often, though, the assumptions about knowledge, disciplinarity, and written representation that underlie the conventions of graduate-level texts are left unexamined—or unmentioned. In the current "crisis" atmosphere, teachers could easily be more likely to expend more

If writing is a social activity, something done in relation with others, and if writing is improved through processes of revisiting, revising, and reflection, then who decides which others we are authorized to cooperate with, and who decides what kinds of cooperation are acceptable?

effort searching for textual "crimes" than educating themselves and their students.

Donald McCabe and Gary Pavela make a compelling argument for teacher responsibility in promoting academic integrity. They write, "faculty members have primary responsibility for designing the educational environment and experience.... [I]t is important that faculty model, as well as clarify, desired standards" (2004, 14). What does this mean in terms of graduate student writing? First and foremost, it means that we must recognize that it is not only the responsibility of writing teachers and professional writing consultants to do the kind of acculturation work I have described. What the so-called crisis in academic integrity tells us is that writing is central to academic work and it is, therefore, the responsibility of the entire academic and administrative community on campus to establish, maintain, and support courses and programs that meet the challenges faced by grad students as they develop into professionals. Faculty can, if given to proper administrative support (such as professional development opportunities), increase their efforts to incorporate writing—and discussions of writing—into their courses in order to: 1) familiarize students with acceptable writing and research practices; 2) familiarize themselves with their students' writing; and 3) clearly establish the connections between the generic conventions and constraints of research writing and relevant disciplinary expectations and practices.

If, as John Thomas Farrell argues, writing consultants (and, likewise, teachers) are responsible for establishing and maintaining "ethical adult, professional relationships" (1996, 1) with graduate students, then teachers must offer instruction in graduate student writing *as colleagues* in whom graduate students can place their trust to acculturate them properly. Of course, graduate students are often teachers themselves, and thus they find themselves in a particular situation: they must learn from their professors and advisors at the same time they are in the position to model behaviors for their undergraduate students. Thus, what is ultimately at stake is the production of new generations of scholars whose research practices are firmly grounded in the principles of academic integrity, who are fully equipped with the knowledge and teaching skills required to train the next generation and understand the weight of the responsibility to do so.

As teachers, before we think "academic dishonesty" we should be thinking "teaching opportunity." At the bottom of any effort to foster an atmosphere of academic integrity is the establishment of an ethical relationship between teacher and student. More so than in undergraduate education, the opportunity to forge collegial relationships with graduate students abounds for faculty, since at the graduate level teachers and students typically work closely together. Rather than being constantly on the lookout for the naughty child with a hand in the cookie jar, teachers, writing consultants, students, and administrators can work together to ensure that students receive the education they need in order to succeed as ethically minded scholars and teachers. To pass that responsibility on to Turnitin.com or writing instructors alone is to abdicate the most basic responsibility we have in creating a community of honesty, trust, fairness, respect, and responsibility: to be excellent teachers, mentors, and colleagues who care more about learning than policing.

Notes

1. "Fabrication, falsification, or misrepresentation of data, results, sources for papers or reports; in clinical practice, as in reporting experiments, measurements, statistical analyses, tests, or other studies never performed; manipulating or altering data or other manifestations of research to achieve a desired result; selective reporting, including the deliberate suppression of conflicting or unwanted data.... Expropriation or abuse of ideas and preliminary data obtained during the process of editorial or peer review of work submitted to journals, or in proposals for funding by agency panels or by internal University committees" (Syracuse University, 2005).

2. The Center for Academic Integrity, formerly at Duke University's Kenan Institute for Ethics, has moved during the publication of this volume. The Center is now hosted by the Rutland Institute for Ethics at Clemson University. The Center can still be found online at the same address: http://www.academicintegrity.org .

Works Cited

Camp, R. (1996). New views of measurement and new models for writing assessment. In E. M. White, W. Lutz, & S. Kamusikiri (Eds.), *Assessment of writing: Politics, policies, practices* (pp. 135-147). New York: MLA.

Council of Writing Program Administrators. (2003). *Defining and avoiding plagiarism: WPA statement on best policies.* Available at http://wpacouncil.org/positions/plagiarism.html.

Farrell, J. T. (1996, March). *The writing center professional and graduate students: Developing an ethical paradigm.* Paper presented at the annual meeting of the Conference on College Composition and Communication. Available through the EDRS database.

Howard, R. M. (1999) *Standing in the shadow of giants: Plagiarists, authors, collaborators.* Stamford, CT: Ablex.

McCabe, D. L., & Pavela, G. (2004). Ten (updated) principles of academic integrity: How faculty can foster student honesty. *Change, 36*(3), 10-15.

Syracuse University, Office of Academic Integrity. (2005). Syracuse University academic integrity policies and procedures. Available at http://provost.syr.edu.academicintegrity_office.asp.

Academic Integrity
in the Mentoring Relationship
A Sampling of Relevant Issues

Ryan Thibodeau

FOR MOST GRADUATE STUDENTS, the cultivation of close working relationships with skilled mentors is key to training. These relationships frequently represent the central route through which essential professional competencies are acquired. Moreover, the overall quality of the training experience is in large measure determined by the extent to which the mentor and graduate student can mutually fashion a fruitful working alliance. This working alliance is, in turn, facilitated by the successful negotiation of a variety of academic integrity issues that impinge on the relationship. Three academic integrity issues assume the central focus of this chapter: (1) determination of authorship credit on collaborative projects, (2) role issues and establishment of boundaries, and (3) resolution of conflicts related to these or other areas. For each, the issues are briefly discussed, their relevance to academic integrity is made explicit, and recommendations are offered.

Determination of Authorship Credit on Collaborative Projects

From a graduate student's perspective, collaborative research involving a faculty mentor can be enormously rewarding. These collaborations allow students to capitalize on the mentor's wealth of experience and expertise, and skills acquired in these partnerships form the foundation of success in graduate school and beyond. Collaborators can offer each other moral support and encouragement as they tackle the difficult and demanding tasks of original research (Mendenhall & Higbee, 1982). The old adage "two heads are better than one" seems entirely relevant to collaborative work in academe. Coming together to solve problems and advance a scholarly agenda may lead to greater yields than either mentors or graduate students could produce alone. Of course, collaborative research in graduate school often involves numerous others aside from one's primary mentor. Research teams in many disciplines (particularly the medical sciences) can be quite large indeed. Learning to cooperate with the various personalities that compose the collaborative team can itself be a valuable training exercise.

When the collaborative work is complete and the manuscript prepared for publication, major contributors to the project appear in the authors' byline. The byline serves two principal functions. First, it establishes accountability (Reichelt, James, & Milne, 1998). The individuals whose names appear in the byline attest to the integrity of the product and endorse the conclusions, along with the specific means used to reach them, presented in the manuscript. It is the task of the authors to address questions, criticisms, or controversies that derive from a public appraisal of the product. Second, authorship credit serves as a reward for executing professional duties essential to completion of the project. In academe, it is widely known that the reward function of authorship is quite lucrative. For faculty, the quantity and quality of authored publications is central to tenure and promotion, salary increases, and opportunities to procure research funding (Costa & Gatz, 1992; Holaday & Yost, 1995; Louw & Fouché, 1999; Sandler & Russell, 2005). For graduate students, authorship enhances competitiveness for internships, postdoctoral fellowships, and academic and nonacademic positions (Hopko, Hopko, and Morris, 1999).

The overall quality of the graduate student's training experience is in large measure determined by the extent to which the mentor and student can mutually fashion a fruitful working alliance facilitated by the successful negotiation of academic integrity issues.

Given these high stakes, determining authorship credit on collaborative projects can be a delicate task. What types of contributions to the project merit authorship designation? Which contributors should be included as authors? In what order should contributors' names appear in the byline? The latter question is meaningful in light of the fact that, in many disciplines, authorship order communicates information regarding the magnitude of contributions set forth by collaborators. As such, publications in which one's name appears first (known as *first-authored* publications) are particularly coveted (e.g., Marco & Schmidt, 2004).

Determining authorship credit on collaborative projects involving one or more faculty mentors can be particularly fraught with problems. First, there exists an inherent asymmetry in power and influence between faculty and graduate students (Fine & Kurdek, 1993). Thus, the potential for faculty to abuse power in ways that exploit students, such as claiming more credit than is warranted, has been highlighted (Kwok 2005; Wagena 2005). Short of egregious exploitation, graduate students may be all too willing to defer to faculty in making decisions regarding authorship listing. By failing to advocate fully their own interests, graduate students may find themselves shortchanged with respect to authorship credit. On the other hand, the power asymmetry may instead result in overgenerosity on the part of mentors. That is, mentors may be inclined to ascribe *greater* authorship credit to students than is warranted by actual contributions. This may be particularly true of senior faculty (Over & Smallman, 1973; Costa & Gatz, 1992; Zuckerman, 1968), for whom pressure to produce first-authored publications diminishes.

Relevance to academic integrity. How do these authorship issues relate to academic integrity? First, one could envision instances in which failure to negotiate properly the potentially rocky terrain of authorship determination compromises each of the core values central to academic integrity: honesty, trust, fairness, respect, responsibility (Center for Academic Integrity, 1999).[1] Second, basic procedures for determining authorship credit are outlined in ethics codes and guidelines in numerous disciplines. Thus, failure to carefully and responsibly consider authorship issues would, as a matter of necessity, involve questions of academic and ethical integrity.

Recommendations. First, graduate students should familiarize themselves with discipline-specific policies and procedures used to determine the awarding and designation of authorship credit early in their graduate careers. As mentioned, many disciplines have ethics codes (e.g., American Psychological Association, 2002; American Sociological Association, 1999) that are instructive with respect to authorship determination or other widely accepted guidelines (see, e.g., International Committee of Medical Journal Editors, 1991) that are typically invoked. Such guidelines generally outline contributions that merit authorship and those that do not, and set forth procedures for determining authorship order. Clearly, such guidelines are not without limitations. Some writers (e.g., Keith-Spiegel & Koocher, 1985) have argued that many sets of guidelines use ambiguous language that invites competing interpretations. Limitations notwithstanding, these guidelines serve as useful heuristics to consult when determining authorship credit.

Second, the decision-making process should begin early in the project to minimize the likelihood of later conflict when the manuscript is ready for submission. Graduate students should insist on being active participants in these discussions. Learning to negotiate authorship issues should be viewed as a pivotal training task, and as such, faculty mentors can take the lead in instructing students as to the appropriate procedures used in making such determinations. In this training context, discussions of authorship should include the following: (1) outlining tasks that need to be completed during the course of the project, (2) determining which project personnel will complete these tasks, (3) discussing which contributions merit authorship credit, as per accepted standards in the discipline, and (4) tentatively determining authorship order. Finally, authorship issues should be revisited often as the project unfolds. Original research is a dynamic and always evolving enterprise. Key tasks that were unanticipated at the outset of project planning invariably arise and require attention. Strategies for determining authorship must be sufficiently malleable to accommodate the fluid nature of the work.

Roles and Boundaries

For many graduate students, the mentor-student relationship is unlike most others encountered previously in one's academic career. Undergraduate training provides a stark contrast. For undergraduates, many relationships with faculty are rather distant. Most one-to-one interactions between undergraduates and faculty are limited to brief chats before or after class or the occasional visit to office hours. Moreover, faculty typically adopt a single role: teacher. In graduate school, however, relationships with faculty mentors are generally much closer and more collegial. Similar to any good relationship, a prosperous mentor-student relationship is built upon a foundation of trust, mutual respect, and honesty. Furthermore, the mentor-student relationship is inherently marked by multiple roles

> *The strongest mentoring relationships are marked by the mentor's execution of multiple roles. Thus, some degree of boundary blurring is expected. In spite of this, a healthy mentoring relationship is bounded, intellectually and personally or emotionally.*

(Johnson & Nelson, 1999). Mentors commonly enact any or all of the following roles: academic advisor, role model, career counselor, course instructor, advocate, coach, and friend. Indeed, the strongest mentoring relationships are marked by the mentor's execution of multiple roles (Johnson & Huwe, 2002). Thus, some degree of boundary blurring is expected. In spite of this, a healthy mentoring relationship is bounded, to a greater or lesser extent, (1) intellectually (Hockey 1994) and (2) personally or emotionally.

Intellectual boundaries. A high degree of autonomy is expected of graduate students pursuing advanced degrees in any given field of study. The academy demands that graduate students' work substantially reflects their own ideas, efforts, insights, and conclusions. These demands are particularly salient with respect to the Ph.D. dissertation, which, by definition, reflects the original work of the student. This is not to say, of course, that students are prohibited from seeking guidance to complete their work. To the contrary, the mentoring relationship rests on the assumption that students, as novice scholars, require some degree of expert supervision to produce quality work and advance in their studies. The question, then, is rather *how much* guidance is appropriate to provide. This question bears directly on the issue of intellectual boundaries, which entail limits on the volume, specificity, depth, and quality of the mentor's involvement in the student's academic affairs (Hockey, 1994). In general, effective intellectual boundaries permit reasonable guidance and assistance from mentors, but do not permit overinvolvement or "hand holding." Students are entitled to expect a mentor's helpful input, but should not expect hyper-vigilant hovering over their academic affairs. In the end, such a strategy would do a great disservice to students anyhow, as it would be hard for graduate students truly to mature as scholars under such conditions.

Personal or emotional boundaries. Personal relationships with faculty mentors are not inherently problematic. However, certain types of personal relationships are troublesome. Moreover, excessive emotional involvement in the mentoring relationship (on the part of mentors or students) can lead to problems.

First, obviously, sexual relationships between faculty mentors and graduate students provide a clear example of personal or emotional overinvolvement. Although such relationships are not always explicitly forbidden in professional codes of ethics or institutional policies, they can pose serious threats to academic integrity and should thus be strongly discouraged. Syracuse University's sexual harassment policy "strongly discourages [faculty from pursuing] sexual relationships with graduate students and any subordinate whose work the [faculty member] supervises" (Syracuse University, 2006). It goes on to say that if a sexual relationship does develop, alternative arrangements for evaluation and monitoring of the student's work must be made. Given the closeness of the mentor-student relationship, the development of sexual attraction is not uncommon (Tabachnick, Keith-Spiegel, & Pope, 1991). However, translating attraction into action comes with a variety of potentially untoward consequences that may not be sufficiently acknowledged at the outset of the encounter.

Second, in instances where the mentor supervises multiple graduate students, positive personal feelings for any one of them should not lead to a "favored child" situation (Plaut, 1993). Such an arrangement could lead to greater academic and professional opportunities, more favorable evaluations, more one-to-one mentoring time, and so on. Of course, all of the above may very reasonably be based upon merit. That is, if Student A's effort and motivation far exceeds Student B's, then Student A should expect to reap greater rewards and a more satisfactory relationship with the mentor. The point is that personal amity, per se, should not be used to justify inequitable treatment of students. The mentor must be vigilant in detecting such states of affairs and promptly eliminating them if they develop.

Relevance to academic integrity. Violation of intellectual boundaries implicates academic integrity because it rightly invites serious questions as to the student's ownership of work that is, in fact, substantially based upon another's contributions. With respect to personal or emotional boundaries, if close personal relationships result in the provision of professionally lucrative benefits to the student that are (1) unavailable to other students and (2) not substantially based upon merit, this unquestionably brings academic integrity concerns to the fore.

Recommendations. First, a candid discussion of roles and boundaries should be carried out early in the mentoring relationship. Mentors should clearly delineate the roles that they intend to adopt, the boundaries that they intend to erect, and a rationale for both. Moreover, mentors should clearly communicate what is expected of their students. This helps novice trainees begin to craft their own identities as graduate students and clarifies the nature of their roles in the mentoring relationship. Failure to do this may produce role confusion, boundary blurring, and, ultimately, an impaired mentoring relationship.

Second, roles evolve over the course of the mentoring relationship. For instance, early in a graduate student's career, the mentor's role as academic advisor is primary. The mentor advises on course selection, negotiating the departmental milieu, and so on. Later, the roles of career counselor and friend increase in prominence. Both mentors and students should carefully track the evolution of the mentoring relationship and critically examine whether changing roles and shifting boundaries are problematic. Is it the case, for example, that a mentor's expanding role as friend disrupts her or his ability to provide objective feedback regarding student performance?

Finally, it has been suggested that formal training to prepare junior mentors for their diverse assortment of roles in the mentoring relationship may reduce concerns related to role confusion and boundary violations (Johnson & Huwe, 2002). Such training may assist in alerting junior mentors as to what lies ahead in the business of mentoring and may enhance the overall efficacy of mentors' scholarly supervision of students.

Conflict Resolution

All relationships, even rock solid ones, are characterized by occasional disputes. These disputes need not represent insurmountable roadblocks. Successful resolution of conflicts in the mentoring relationship can ultimately strengthen, not weaken, the bond. Unsuccessful resolution can, in certain instances, derail a graduate career. Thus, the importance of an effective conflict resolution strategy cannot be overstated. Recommendations as to key ingredients of such a strategy are offered below. However, consideration of an exhaustive set of procedures for resolving conflicts in the mentoring relationship is beyond the scope of this chapter. The reader is referred to Klomparens, Beck, Brockman, and Larson (2004) for a more comprehensive treatment of this important issue.

Relevance to academic integrity. Failure to address conflicts in the mentoring relationship in a timely and responsible fashion may lead to academic integrity problems by fostering a generally hostile climate in which to conduct one's academic affairs. This hostile climate may, in turn, increase the likelihood of engaging in scholarly conduct that threatens the core values of academic integrity. Indeed, some readers may know of situations in which disputes in the mentoring relationship have prompted conduct on the part of mentors or students that is questionable in its ethical soundness.

Recommendations. First, it is essential for students to avoid stewing in the emotional upset of a budding conflict. Permitting a conflict to simmer long enough will eventually yield unmanageable friction that can only impair the mentoring relationship. Ill will, resentment, and hurt feelings are common consequences of a failure to directly address conflict in a timely fashion.

Second, graduate students should be direct and honest, yet tactful and respectful, in addressing conflict with mentors. A failure to communicate directly one's thoughts and feelings, thereby precluding an open airing of relevant issues, often renders a conflict unsolvable.

Third, it is important for graduate students to seek advice in managing conflicts with a mentor. More senior students can frequently offer a wealth of valuable insights which can be brought to bear on resolving a conflict. In addition, many departments have ombudspersons whose principal role is to assist in resolving conflicts. Graduate students should not be timid in consulting these or other individuals who can offer a fair, objective appraisal of the problem and possible resolution strategies.

Concluding Remarks

Graduate school is an exciting time of intellectual and professional growth, and mentoring relationships are vitally important in this process. For the mentoring relationship to truly thrive, graduate students and mentors must build their bond on a foundation of strong academic integrity. Careful attention to the issues outlined here may facilitate this important endeavor and, in turn, enhance the overall quality of the training experience.

Notes

1. The Center for Academic Integrity, formerly at Duke University's Kenan Institute for Ethics, has moved during the publication of this volume. The Center is now hosted by the Rutland Institute for Ethics at Clemson University. The Center can still be found online at the same address: http://www.academicintegrity.org

Works Cited

American Sociological Association. (1999). Code of ethics and policies and procedures of the ASA Committee on Professional Ethics. Available at http://www.asanet.org

American Psychological Association. (2002). Ethical principles of psychologists and code of conduct. *American Psychologist, 57,* 1060-1073.

Center for Academic Integrity. (1999). The fundamental values of academic integrity. Kenan Institute for Ethics, Duke University. Available at http://www.academicintegrity.org/fundamental_values_project/index.php

Costa, M. M., & Gatz, M. (1992). Determination of authorship credit in published dissertations. *Psychological Science, 3,* 354-357.

Fine, M. A., & Kurdek, L. A. (1993). Reflections on determining authorship credit and authorship order on faculty-student collaborations. *American Psychologist, 48,* 1141-1147.

Hockey, J. (1994). Establishing boundaries: Problems and solutions in managing the Ph.D. supervisor's role. *Cambridge Journal of Education, 24,* 293-305.

Holaday, M., & Yost, T. E. (1995). Authorship credit and ethical guidelines. *Counseling and Values, 40,* 24-31.

Hopko, D. R., Hopko, S. D., & Morris, T. L. (1999). The application of behavioral contracting to authorship status. *Behavior Therapist, 22,* 93-95.

International Committee of Medical Journal Editors. (1991). Uniform requirements for manuscripts submitted to biomedical journals. *New England Journal of Medicine, 324,* 424-428.

Johnson, W. B., & Huwe, J. M. (2002). Toward a typology of mentorship dysfunction in graduate school. *Psychotherapy: Theory/Research/Practice/Training, 39,* 44-55.

Johnson, W. B., & Nelson, N. (1999). Mentor-protégé relationships in graduate training: Some ethical concerns. *Ethics and Behavior, 9,* 189-210.

Keith-Spiegel, P., & Koocher, G. P. (1985). *Ethics in psychology: Professional standards and cases.* New York: Random House.

Klomparens, K. L., Beck, J. P., Brockman, J., & Larson, R. S. (2004). Setting expectations and resolving conflicts in graduate education. *Journal for Higher Education Strategists, 2,* 21-37.

Kwok, L. S. (2005). The White Bull effect: Abusive coauthorship and publication parasitism. *Journal of Medical Ethics, 31,* 554-556.

Louw, D. A., & Fouché, J. B. (1999). Authorship credit in supervisor-student collaboration: Assessing the dilemma in psychology. *South African Journal of Psychology, 29,* 145-148.

Marco, C. A., & Schmidt, T. A. (2004). Who wrote this paper? Basics of authorship and ethical issues. *Academic Emergency Medicine, 11,* 76-77.

Mendenhall, M., & Higbee, K. L. (1982). Psychology and the scientist: XLVIII. Recent trends in multiple authorships in psychology. *Psychological Reports, 51,* 1019-1022.

Over, R., & Smallman, S. (1973). Maintenance of individual visibility in publication of collaborative research in psychology. *American Psychologist, 28,* 161-166.

Plaut, S. M. (1993). Boundary issues in teacher-student relationships. *Journal of Sex and Marital Therapy, 19,* 210-219.

Reichelt, F. K., James, I. A., & Milne, D. L. (1998). Credit where credit's due: Guidelines on authorship. *Behavioural and Cognitive Psychotherapy, 26,* 339-344.

Sandler, J. C., & Russell, B. L. (2005). Faculty-student collaborations: Ethics and satisfaction in authorship credit. *Ethics and Behavior, 15,* 65-80.

Syracuse University (2006). *Sexual harassment policies and procedures.* Syracuse University, Online Administrative Policies Manual. Available at http://sumweb.syr.edu/ir/apm/Vphrgr/humres/appsex.html.

Tabachnick, B. G., Keith-Spiegel, P., & Pope, K. S. (1991). Ethics of teaching: Beliefs and behaviors of psychologists as educators. *American Psychologist, 46,* 506-515.

Wagena, E. J. (2005). The scandal of unfair behaviour of senior faculty. *Journal of Medical Ethics, 31,* 308.

Zuckerman, H. A. (1968). Patterns of name ordering among authors of scientific papers: A study of social symbolism and its ambiguity. *American Journal of Sociology, 74,* 276-291.

III

THE PEOPLE BEHIND THE POLICIES

THE WORD "POLICY," like "police," has a root that sinks it deep into the soil of Western languages. Familiar in the Greek as *polis*, the foundation of policy is, like a Greek city-state, the model of order and conduct. If one were to return to the fifth century BCE and to Plato's *Republic*–a translation from the Greek *politeia*–a scholar would find that the ideal city-state is one based on everyone performing his role in order and harmony with each other, staying within his birthright so as to reduce conflict. While the ideal *politeia* may bring peace, it does so at the cost of a rigid structure of behavior that allows for little originality. Plato believed few were capable of responsible creativity, and so the majority was assigned narrow roles to be lived expertly.

This mostly faceless order is sustained in contemporary understandings of "policy." Policies allow authorities to operate with indemnity so that other guiding systems, such as personal revenge, do not take hold. While it is tacitly agreed that policy serves society well most of the time, people do still scapegoat those who hold authority positions, even if they are not directly responsible for the policy. The blame game goes around, and it seems like everyone is looking for a person responsible for upsetting the social order, as if to say that if one could find the guilty party, root her out, and make an example of her, then the institution would again return to some static, well-ordered *polis* with everyone operating within his or her own bounds.

This section takes up this dynamic of the personal within the political. It traces how the responsibility of academic integrity is situated within individual choices and yet spreads through trajectories of power that have little to do with individuals. We present this section not only to personalize policy but also to *de*personalize it–to mark how academic integrity is not as simple as "cheating" or "policing," a contest of the lawmakers versus the lawbreakers.

The chapters that follow offer rich testimony from people at the intersections of power with varying levels of accountability and responsibility. As editors, we see this section as handing over to readers lenses that give access to others' perspectives that would otherwise be invisible or perhaps little understood. Kimberly Ray looks back on her first TA experience in hopes of showing a different way for other TAs. Undergraduate Lucy McGregor addresses her TA directly and gives insight into what it's like to be a student athlete. David Bozak, with years of experience in administration, shows how to untangle the complex of rules and feelings around what comes across as a moral indignation.

Two special contributions highlight unique roles in the academic integrity circle. The first is by Ruth Federman Stein, interim direction of the Academic Integrity Office at Syracuse University. In her first-person narrative, she describes her work and the goals of an office that is responsible for interpreting a university-wide policy on academic integrity that effects more than 20,000 students, faculty, and administrators. The second is by Sidney Greenblatt, titled "Culture and Academic Norms." In this article, Greenblatt opens U.S.-trained scholars to thinking that cultures perform "academic" and "integrity" in distinct ways. As the last contributor to this section on the people behind the policies, Greenblatt argues that policies themselves have unique histories and need to be regarded as contextual. We hope that the chapters together show the continued need for policies and the value of dialogue around them. As any scholar of Plato knows, the *Republic* isn't merely a list of laws for ruling an ideal city but is itself a dialogue conducted between Socrates and his friends on the nature of justice and virtue.

A Reflection on Plagiarism
by a First-Time Instructor

Kimberly Ray

PREPARING FOR my first semester of teaching, I devoted much of my time to my syllabi, PowerPoint slides, and course calendars. Like most instructors on a university campus, I included a statement that addressed academic integrity. To make my efforts more pronounced, I used the official statement from the University. In my mind this was just a formality; I didn't think for a second that I would have an incident of plagiarism in my first semester of teaching. How naïve I was!

It struck me as I was grading papers in my office after a challenging class: two of the students' papers were indistinguishable. Even the typos were the same. The only difference was the names at the top of the paper. Now I was presented with a difficult decision: report the incident, or handle it myself. I had two days until I saw the students again, so I needed to make a decision soon. The freshmen offenders had very different classroom presences. Student A was respectful and attended and participated in class regularly. Student B was disrespectful, lazy, and had poor attendance. Student A turned the assignment in during class, while Student B came to my office 30 minutes after class and handed the assignment in late. This brought to light an interesting dilemma. Did I report the incident and set into motion events that would follow these students' academic careers, even for Student A, who otherwise seemed like a "good" student and might just have made a dumb decision? How seriously would I be taken by the students if I handled it on my own and with minimal consequences (compared to the ramifications of officially documenting the suspected offense)?

Weighing my options and taking into account the seriousness of academic integrity, I decided to give them both a failing grade for the assignment. I was teaching a course that focused primarily on introducing freshmen to college customs and expectations, along with promoting skills for lifelong learning. I felt as though this could be a learning experience for the students, and told them to consider this as their one and only "break." In addition, I took the opportunity to emphasize the issues of academic integrity in a university setting during the next class meeting. I discussed the definition of academic integrity, our university's administrative policies, and the grave consequences of reported incidents.

Reflecting back now on how I handled the situation, I did not make the right decision in the beginning. The same students committed a similar offense during a quiz close to the end of the semester. Due to lack of classroom space, students had to sit right next to each other. (In my ideal situation the students would sit at least one seat apart.) As I was proctoring the quiz, I noticed Student B lowering his cap and turning his head toward Student A's paper. After this quick glance, he swiftly wrote down an answer on his paper. I nonchalantly continued my walk around the room and when I reached the suspected offender's desk (Student B), I glanced down at his paper and at Student A's paper; the answers were the same! I waited until I was in my office reviewing the quizzes later that day to assess the issue. All the answers on the two quiz papers were the same. By this time I had had it! It is *suggested* by the faculty handbook to discuss the incident with the student before formal action is taken. Since I was on campus only one day a week, had extended a previous warning to the two students, and had already spent considerable time addressing the first incident, I did not feel it necessary to call the students in before I sent documentation to the administration; I also had the support of the associate dean in this matter.

Observing the students' disrespectful behavior and lack of motivation made me want to go back in time to change my decision not to "nail their butts to the wall" in the first place. If I had documented the first incident according to the suggestions of the faculty handbook, I might not have had to have spend additional time dealing with this offense a second time around. As a young instructor, I understood that adjustment to college could be quite challenging, but I might have been too lenient because of my sympathy. I have decided that, in that particular situation, the best decision would have been to document the occurrence and hand it over to the administration. I believe that everyone has a "wake-up" call during the early days of his or her academic career, and maybe this could have been one for these two students. Unfortunately, they got theirs too late. By the end of the semester, both students had failed miserably in all of their classes, and they eventually had to be dismissed by the end of the academic year.

Letter to My Teaching Assistant
Academic Integrity from the Student Athlete's Perspective

Lucy McGregor

DEAR TA,

The purpose of this letter is to give you—teaching assistants and faculty—an insight into a student's life and to help shed light on the student's perspective on academic life, in particular athletes' academic integrity. Athletes are one group of students that face a hard time managing their time due to their academic and sporting commitments. I want to share with you the factors that may play a role in students' and student-athletes' choice to plagiarize. As you could probably guess, the biggest of these is time constraints. But plagiarizing is also tempting and easy to do when assignments are easy and do not require much outside thinking. I thought that by sharing some of my perspectives, we could problem-solve on how to help each other out so that I'm less tempted to cheat and you can see how much I care about my learning.

On a personal note, I am a junior transfer student here in Syracuse for an academic year from the University of Canterbury in Christchurch, New Zealand. I am majoring in psychology, and hope to go to go on to do postgraduate study in clinical psychology eventually. I have actually gained quite a different perspective from studying in America. It is quite different from what it is like back in New Zealand. Being a student athlete is one thing that I have found hard to adjust to. I have found it difficult mainly because of the intense nature of Division I sports. It almost feels as though we are professional athletes because of the huge time commitment that is required, the pressures to perform well, all the scholarship money that goes into sports, and the way that it seems to take over one's life. Coming from New Zealand, where we do not have anything like the NCAA competition, this was a big culture shock for me, and one that took adjusting to. I have played sports very competitively at home in the past, but it is different here because of the very nature of the NCAA: the fact that it is a university-based competition means that you have to be a student and an athlete at the same time. One does not exist without the other. At home, the people I play sports with come from different backgrounds, and when we play we represent only our sports team, not like here, where you are not only a representative of the field hockey team, you are a representative of Syracuse University, too.

The academic side of things is different also. In New Zealand, the learning is more autonomous. I was quite shocked to come here and have attendance taken in lectures, and points deducted if you missed a certain number. In one class, the teacher offered bonus points for attending, which seems even sillier than requiring attendance. In New Zealand, you could skip all your lectures and no one would notice, or care for that matter! The emphasis is placed really on the content. If you miss class, you miss content and that has its effect. A bigger emphasis is also placed on midterm exams than at home too, where it's all about the final exam. I don't know why the difference, really, or if more or less people cheat in these different systems. What I do know from my experience at home is that there I am responsible for my own learning, and my grade there reflects what I know, whereas here you are not only getting a grade for what you know, but for how diligent you are with your learning as well.

It seems obvious that students plagiarize because of time constraints. I am sure that almost everyone in their university career has had that horrible, hopeless feeling before a test, knowing that they haven't reviewed all the material that they should have. Perhaps there is one certain thing that you can't quite remember—a formula, a theorist's name, how many calories are in one gram of protein—so why not just write it on your arm, or stick an inconspicuous piece of paper on the brim of your cap; surely no one would notice, would they? Because athletes have extra commitments and need to have good grades to play, it might be assumed that athletes might want to cheat more. Athletes' training schedules are full-on, to say the least. NCAA rules stipulate that all Division I teams shall train for no more than four hours per day during the season, with one mandatory day off per week (football and basketball may have exceptions to this rule). Thus, an athlete is permitted to train for 20 hours per week. This does not include traveling time, and time spent competing, time spent in the training room stretching and getting treatment before and after trainings and games. Thus, the 20 hours per week probably works out to be many, many more hours when one includes all the other mandatory engagements an athlete must commit to. In the off-season, athletes are still required to train a lot as well. The field hockey team, for example, is scheduled to train every weekday for four-hour sessions, with perhaps another one-hour session on Sunday evenings. This is not a light commitment, considering that student-athletes have to organize their studying schedules around their training times, often putting their sporting commitments before academics. Hence plagiarism and cheating become more of an option when there is not enough time to spend on academics.

Furthermore, in order to be in keeping with NCAA rules, athletes must pass a certain number of classes so they will be considered full-time students. Thus, there is extra pressure to succeed in subjects, because if one doesn't pass enough and fails too many classes to be considered a full-time student, he or she will no longer be eligible to play. Particular sports also have specific stipulations as to what is required by their athletes. For field hockey, one has to have a GPA of 2.8 or above to stay out of "tables." Tables requires that student athletes go to the academic center (located at the Manley Field House) and study there for ten hours every week (there is a computer system there that tallies athletes' hours spent in tables, and reports go out to coaches every week to ensure athletes are going). Going to tables isn't exactly a favorite pastime of athletes; to say the least, it is a chore to have to spend a further 10 hours a week studying at tables. When athletes spend upwards of 20 hours a week training, plus time spent in class, plus ten hours a week in tables, it does not leave much, if any, free time. Furthermore, there is quite a social aspect to tables, because there are lots of athletes in there, from not only your team, but also other sports, and so a lot of people actually do not get very much work done! This not only defeats the purpose of making tables mandatory, but it leaves the athletes with more homework to do and less time to do it in. Thus they are pressured to keep their GPAs high enough in order to stay out of tables—another added factor that could lead to cheating and plagiarism.

If a TA succeeded in making the learning environment fun and stimulating, and giving assignments and tests on topics that people were interested in, the urge for people to plagiarize and cheat would lessen.

Another factor, perhaps not so obvious, that may contribute to plagiarizing in particular is the nature of assignments themselves. I know that there are some courses that have used the same assignments for years, and so for people to do well in these assignments, they need only obtain copies of people's past work and copy these! Personally, I have been most tempted to plagiarize when I have been assigned very easy projects, ones that don't really require any free thinking on my part.

I will elaborate. For one essay we were asked to write briefly (1,500 words) on the historical background to a particular ethnic conflict. While this was indeed a valid and interesting topic, the nature of the assignment was such that it was too easy to simply access a very basic history book, or *Wikipedia,* or something similar, and virtually copy and paste what these sources were saying. Rather than simply asking us to regurgitate facts, why not ask us to relate this ethnic conflict to another similar conflict and compare and contrast these? Assignments that require no personal interpretation, opinion, or free thinking, leave themselves wide open to plagiarism.

I can imagine that being a TA would not be an easy job, and part of the difficulty would be to try to tailor your classes so they suit a group of students with very different backgrounds, learning styles, and lifestyles. Personally, I think that if a TA succeeded in making the learning environment fun and stimulating, and gave assignments and tests on topics that people were interested in, the urge for people to plagiarize and cheat would lessen. As mentioned, the pressure on students, and in particular student athletes, to succeed academically is great, and therefore the practice of plagiarism and cheating may emerge because of this. If a TA is willing to help people who are having difficulty academically, and actively encourages students to make the most of services such as office hours and extra study sessions, then the students will probably feel less pressured, and hopefully seek help if they are feeling overwhelmed. All people, including TAs, face huge time constraints, so I don't think that exceptions should be made for student athletes. I do believe, however, that it does help student athletes to know that a TA is willing to help out. Personally, I would not feel the inclination to plagiarize and cheat if I knew that I had a TA whom I could talk to about academics, who would understand my situation being a student athlete, and who would therefore help me with any potential problems I might face with academics and sport.

All people, including TAs, face huge time constraints, so I don't think that exceptions should be made for student athletes. I do believe, however, that it does help student athletes to know that a TA is willing to help out.

Sincerely,
Lucy McGregor

Learn to Hate Dishonesty Without Becoming Emotionally Involved

David Alan Bozak

DR. ELIZABETH KUBLER-ROSS (1969) introduced us to the five stages of grief that terminally ill patients go through—denial, anger, bargaining, depression, and finally acceptance. Dr. Carolyn Foster Segal (2006) presented the seven stages of "plagiarism grief" that students confronted by their misconduct go through—disbelief, denial, astonishment, confusion (parts 1 and 2), plea (parts 1 through 6!), defense, and accusation. There is no doubt that faculty, too, display a wide gamut of emotions when they encounter instances of academic dishonesty. Anger, annoyance, anxiety, depression, frustration, incredulity, regret, resentfulness, resignation, more anger, and more depression—these and other emotions are part of the baggage that goes along with an instructor's experience of "plagiarism grief."

Embracing the emotion of hate (hating the *sin*, mind you, and not the sinner) enables one to avoid the one unacceptable emotional response to encountering plagiarism—acceptance. The energy underlying the emotion is caused by a perceived violation of the social contract the instructor has with the student, a reaction to an apparent rejection of his or her academic duty. It is important not to let misdirected energy interfere with a process that, in the long run, is best for both instructors and students. In order to avoid their own and their students' intense emotions, many faculty members choose to handle the situation on their own, running away from their emotional responses rather than using the energy in a positive way. However, this way of "handling it" reflects the same kind of disbelief, denial, and confusion as is displayed by the accused students. Such avoidance trivializes the misconduct, deprives the student of due process, exposes the instructor to litigation, and is, ultimately, unsatisfying.

Our professional obligation is to be prepared to confront the misconduct rather than merely reacting to—or avoiding—the misconduct. If we are unprepared, our emotional energies are undirected and serve only to agitate us. We should be prepared instead to respond in a manner consistent with campus procedures, and our preparedness should make it much less likely that our responses will catch us off guard or consume us. Knowing the campus policy on academic misconduct allows us to focus our emotional energy in applying policy to the specifics of a particular incident.

To put this in context, consider two plausible scenarios:

Scenario 1. You are a new faculty member (or a new teaching assistant) grading three- to five-page papers for a freshman level introductory course. You are sitting in your office one evening, halfway through both a small pot of coffee and the stack of papers when you come up short from what you have read. You are not sure what it is at first, but then you realize that, by the end of page two of the paper, the writing style has shifted. It does not seem to have the same voice as earlier in the paper. There is also something elegant about a particular phrase. You "Google" the phrase and find thousands of links. The first one is to a page that contains the same paragraph as the paper in your hands, nearly verbatim.

Scenario 2. You are proctoring your first large classroom examination. You have a room more than twice as large as your regular classroom, so students occupy every other seat. You have also created multiple versions of the exam, each on different colored paper, and arranged for another teaching assistant to help you proctor the exam. You are pretty confident that you have things under control. After about forty minutes, as you are walking around the first row, you notice something odd. One of the classroom lights is reflecting off the label of a student's water bottle and it just looks wrong. The student is seated right in the middle of the front row, and as you take a longer look, you notice that there seems to be a great deal of small writing on the *inside* of the label, a place you never expected to look for crib notes.

What is your reaction? In both situations it is likely to be first confusion, then anger mixed with apprehension. Your stomach starts to dance a little bit—you really do not want a confrontation—and you wish that the situation would just go away. In the first scenario, you might think "I have another dozen or more papers to grade, so maybe I should just grade the paper on the basis of the earlier writing, what is likely the more authentic voice, and give the writer a C–." In the second scenario, students are starting to come forward to turn in their exams, and several have questions over the next assignment. You cannot just let them accumulate at the front of the room, disturbing the remaining students, while you figure out what to do with the student with the water bottle. Maybe you just note the exam when it is turned in, and see whether or not that exam has a grade significantly different than other work by that student.

Part of your turmoil is because you are upset by the idea that these students were cheating, and part is because you are not prepared to deal with these situations! You put the paper aside to deal with it later. You make a note of the exam when it is turned in, but the student has packed up the water bottle and left. Ah well, you will deal with it later.

So what happens when "later" comes? The emotional turmoil comes back, perhaps not quite as strong. Now, though, it is time to try to use the energy the emotions have generated to address the problems that are in front of you. You have a professional obligation, not only to deal with the situation rather than ignoring it, but to deal with it in a manner consistent with your campus policy. What is your first step? Make sure you know what that policy is.

Each campus will be different, but it is likely the case that they all have a core commitment to due process. For public colleges and universities due process is mandated by law, by the "due process" clause of the federal constitution. "Since the early 1960s, the concept of procedural due process has been one of the primary legal forces shaping the administration of post-secondary education" (Kaplan & Lee, 1995, 484-5). While private colleges and universities are not bound by the federal due process clause, they may be governed by state sanctions. As Kaplan and Lee illustrate by examining court decisions dating back as far as 1928, the courts have found that to discipline a student, a private college or university must also follow a procedure that is fair and reasonable (497-500). In either event, higher education's philosophy of fair and equitable treatment for all students imposes a philosophic obligation of following a due process procedure to ensure that decisions are not made in an arbitrary or capricious manner. (See, for example, the American Association of University Professors' *Statement on Professional Ethics,* available at http://www.aaup.org/AAUP/pubsres/policydocs/statementonprofessionalethics.htm.)

Higher education's philosophy of fair and equitable treatment for all students imposes a philosophic obligation to following a due process procedure to ensure that decisions are not made in an arbitrary or capricious manner.

We have a pedagogical responsibility to structure our courses and their requirements in a manner that minimizes the opportunities for students to cheat. While some faculty find this to be an onerous chore, not having to address issues of cheating after the fact more than compensates for the up-front effort in course design. But unforeseen incidents may still take place during the course, so what is an instructor who planned ahead to do when problems arise anyway?

Begin by considering what due process asks of us in these circumstances. First and foremost, a student should have the opportunity to explain his or her actions *before* any decision is made regarding the interpretation of those actions. In the plagiarism example used earlier, it is clearly the case that significant material was copied from a website and may have been used without attribution. But why? Was the website listed in the references? Does the student really understand how to cite properly? Correct academic citation is not a skill that most students master in a single basic composition course. Did the student fall victim to a cut-and-paste error that did not get addressed because the paper was completed at four a.m.? A student who otherwise has done solid work without passing the work of others off as his or her own might simply have dropped the ball due to juggling a heavy academic load. Or did the student just not care, and so took whatever steps he or she deemed necessary to submit a minimal paper? In a meeting with a student, an instructor has the opportunity to come to a clear understanding of how the student wrote his or her paper. Only then can a decision be made as to whether or not dishonesty was involved, and, if so, what an appropriate response might be.

Putting the decision in writing allows you to outline for the student the context of his or her behavior and the college's expectations of integrity. Writing such a letter allows you to use your emotional energy to do what you do best: teach.

While the examples used earlier may seem clear-cut, other instances may be more ambiguous. It is incumbent upon faculty to come to a complete understanding of an incident before acting. Certainly, context will influence the decisions made regarding academic or disciplinary penalties. Talk to your chair, mentor, and other faculty in the department. What is the general sense in your department of the seriousness of the particular academic "sin"? What penalties have others applied for similar incidents in the past? That, too, is context that will inform the decision that you make in a specific case.

Finally, you should always notify the student in writing of any decisions that have been made regarding his or her case. Putting the decision in writing allows you to outline for the student the context of his or her behavior and the college's expectations of integrity. The letter should reinforce the college policy. Writing such a letter allows you to use your emotional energy to do what you do best: teach. If the student has made a mechanical or procedural mistake, this is your opportunity to instruct him or her on both proper work processes and the potential penalties for continued mishaps. If the student has deliberately cheated, this is an opportunity to convey to the student just how his or her actions have harmed his or her education, his or her peers' education, and the reputation of the institution's degree. You may feel anger at being victimized, but as Judge Posner (2007) points out, the "principal victims are the plagiarist's student competitors" (106).

What do you do about the student with the water bottle? You have the exam and the student's score was quite high. So was, you discover, his or her first exam score. Your inclination is to fail the student for cheating. But you have no evidence of that assessment, as the student left the room in possession of the water bottle. You did not ask the student if you could look at the water bottle, which would have been a reasonable request. You do not actually know what was on the inside of the label. Though you may be frustrated, there is nothing to be done now but to enter the exam into your gradebook. There is something that you can do *later*, however. Use the energy of the frustration you are experiencing to prepare better an examination environment that further minimizes the opportunity for students to cheat—and to prepare yourself to intervene if you suspect further incidents, even if "intervention" just means asking all of your students to keep their water bottles on the floor.

Hate is a powerful emotion. You hate that a student has cheated—you take it as a personal insult. Maybe you also hate that you might be partially to blame for the situation—perhaps you reused a paper assignment or an exam. Either way, you must accept that that emotional energy is there. We teach because we are passionate about education. We cannot, and should not try to, dismiss the many emotions that we experience as part of that passionate commitment. Instead, we should harness the energy of those emotions to accomplish something positive, making such an experience an educational one for both our students and ourselves.

Works Cited

Kaplan, W. A., & Lee, B. A. (1995). *The law of higher education* (3rd ed.). San Francisco: Jossey-Bass.

Kubler-Ross, E. (1969). *On death and dying.* New York: Macmillan.

Posner, R. A. (2007). *The little book of plagiarism.* New York: Pantheon.

Segal, C. F. (2006, September 15). Copy this. *The Chronicle of Higher Education,* *53*(4), B5.

Academic Integrity from Behind the Administrator's Desk

Ruth Federman Stein

IN JULY 2006, I started working as interim director of Syracuse University's newly established Academic Integrity Office (AIO). The office, in terms of the university's institutional structure, comes under Academic Affairs and is totally separate from Judicial Affairs. The AIO office staff consists of the director and one support staff person. When I began in July, the university's new Academic Policy and Procedures had been written and approved; our job was to implement them.

Patterns

By the end of the fall 2006 semester, 42 violations had been reported to the AIO, a surprisingly small number. Of the 42 reported violations, 37 involved undergraduates and 5 involved graduate students. Twenty-seven of the violations occurred in the College of Arts and Sciences. As the semesters pass, patterns of cheating or plagiarism in particular areas may be identified, and the AIO hopes to support ways to reduce these violations.

Dealing With Academic Integrity Violations

The first year started out very slowly. After several weeks, however, a few violations had been reported, and the numbers increased as the semester progressed. The procedure requires entering each reported violation into a database that only I and my assistant can access. Each student who violates the academic integrity policy for the first time is required to complete academic integrity programming through the AIO. As I worked on the planning for this programming, I decided that it would be best for me to meet individually with students. It didn't seem appropriate to provide generic programming because each student had a slightly different kind of violation or different circumstances surrounding the violation. One-on-one tutorials also maintain confidentiality for everyone, which is an important feature of the policy.

The individual tutorial sessions are an important aspect of my work. Most of the students with whom I meet are honest in admitting what they have done—usually plagiarism. They explain what happened that led them to plagiarize.

Syracuse University's Vice Chancellor and Provost's Committee on Academic Integrity stated in March 2005 that 74% of undergraduate students and 42% of graduate students reported cheating behaviors.

Generally, they are under stress of some sort (crisis at home, deadline pressure) and make a poor decision without considering any of the consequences. In these meetings, the student and I typically discuss how to deal with issues of stress and time management and how to make a better decision the next time that they are under pressure. As we talk, if I have a computer available, I develop a list of behaviors, actions, and tips that they can follow in the future. For example, if students are writing on the computer and looking something up on the Internet—copying and pasting—they should paste the information in using a different color or bold it and immediately put it in quotation marks and cite the Internet source. That way they can't "forget" that this material was taken from another source. I also stress the importance of meeting with their instructors as they are writing papers or going to the Writing Center, especially if they are struggling with their ideas or with the assignment. I've also learned that many students have not mastered the skills of paraphrasing and summarizing; they do not realize that changing a few words in a paragraph is not paraphrasing and that paraphrased material still requires a citation. As we talk, I try to focus ideas and suggestions to meet the particular needs of that student. Improving their writing process should help students make conscious, ethical decisions as they write.

Changing the Culture

Ethical behavior is a troubling issue in American society, as can be seen in how newspaper headlines frequently deal with business and political ethics. Internet scams also make headlines. How do we educate our students to understand that ethical behavior is important, whether it pertains to giving credit in papers for ideas from others, taking a test without cheating, or writing a truthful résumé?

The *Academic Rules and Regulations* at Syracuse University state that all instructors are "responsible for stating in writing course-specific expectations, particularly those regarding use of sources and collaboration" (Syracuse University, 2006, 6). But we need to go beyond that. Instructors should also discuss their integrity expectations in their classes. For example, expectations for working together on reports or projects must be clearly explained so that there are no gray areas for students. Additionally, students are concerned about integrity and want consistency of enforcement. The Syracuse University Vice Chancellor and Provost's Committee on Academic Integrity (VPCAI) found that "students called for faculty to strictly *enforce the current policies* and for *consistent implementation* by all faculty members" (VPCAI, 2005, 183).

To increase awareness, first-year students during the fall 2006 semester received an electronic newsletter from the Office of Orientation and Transition Services that included tips on academic integrity. When the 2007 first-year students entered, part of their orientation included a video about academic integrity and making good decisions under pressure. The Academic Integrity Office also developed a faculty brochure that was sent to all instructors and teaching assistants with information on the instructor's role, best practices, and how to handle and report academic integrity violations.

Changing the culture will not be easy, but if ethical behavior is consistently emphasized and encouraged across the campus, we may hope that everyone will want to—and know better how to—behave in an honest and ethical manner.

Recommendations

As I reflect on my experiences thus far, I've been thinking about what to share with other instructors. When I meet with students in tutorial sessions, it becomes obvious that they make poor, reckless decisions because they are not thinking at all about the consequences of their actions. Even though each instructor is expected to have a written statement of course-specific academic integrity expectations, I would also encourage instructors to discuss ethical behavior expectations with their students. Such discussion may help students to understand why source citation is an important cultural practice and why integrity is an essential part of all research.

Carefully designed assignments can discourage Internet plagiarism. Topics or questions that are framed by course readings or discussion, or assignments that require a specific format or organization, are not as easy to answer in cut-and-paste fashion as more general topics or questions. Requiring a process that involves a series of steps, such as first submitting a thesis or plan for the paper, an annotated bibliography, and a rough draft, can be effective for deterring last-minute papers.

Many students are timid about meeting with their instructors. TAs should encourage or even require students to meet with them during office hours to discuss their paper drafts or issues that arise as they are writing. Another source of help is the Writing Center. Writing consultants can work with students at various stages of the writing process. The Writing Center can also help non-native speakers of English, and some students who are shy about meeting with professors may be more comfortable seeking help this way.

Another issue is the problem of cheating on exams. To emphasize the seriousness of cheating, TAs should speak with their classes about the importance of honest test-taking. They might ask their students if they would feel comfortable with a doctor who cheated on medical exams or an accountant who copied exam answers from another student. TAs should also create an environment in which cheating is difficult or impossible. When giving examinations, essay tests are best but not always feasible; if multiple-choice exams are necessary, create several versions of the exam by changing the order of the questions. Do not permit students to have cell phones or other electronic equipment at their seats, and try to have sufficient space between students. Exam proctors should circulate around the room and make sure that students are not engaging in any kind of cheating.

Requiring a process that involves a series of steps, such as first submitting a thesis or plan for the paper, an annotated bibliography, and a rough draft, can be effective for deterring last-minute papers.

Students also do not realize that signing another student's name for class attendance violates the academic integrity policy, and they are "shocked" when this behavior is caught and reported. TAs responsible for sign-in sheets should include a statement on the sheet that says signing another student as present (forging a signature) violates the academic integrity policy.

Another violation of the policy is submitting the same paper in more than one course without the prior written permission of both instructors. Students may argue that they didn't know this action was against the policy, but that is not a valid excuse. Students are not learning anything new if they submit the same paper twice. They may, however, request permission from the instructor to expand a paper or to develop another aspect of the topic, but they need written permission in advance from both instructors to do this.

When students get caught for plagiarizing or cheating, the AIO tries to use the first violation as an opportunity to teach students about the importance of academic integrity. However, a second violation requires a hearing, and students may be suspended or expelled from the university. Having a university-wide academic integrity policy is no guarantee that unethical behavior will stop, but I want to encourage all TAs and instructors to emphasize the importance of ethical behavior in their disciplines. If instructors make clear to students their expectations regarding academic integrity, and if they consistently enforce the university's academic integrity policy, I believe that, over time, we will see a shift in student behavior.

Works Cited

Syracuse University (2006). General and undergraduate academic rules and regulations. *Syracuse University bulletin. Undergraduate course catalog, 2006-2007.* Syracuse, NY: author.

Vice Chancellor and Provost's Committee on Academic Integrity. (2005, March). *Research findings.* Syracuse, NY: Syracuse University.

Culture and Academic Norms

An Exploration of the Import of Cultural Difference on
Asian Students' Understanding of American
Approaches to Plagiarism

Sidney L. Greenblatt

Introduction

This short chapter looks at elements of Chinese, and more broadly Asian, history and culture to challenge the idea that academic norms are universally understood and that cheating represents a deliberate attempt to beat the system and reap an advantage. In order to challenge that idea, I will focus on Asian, particularly Chinese, concepts that lie at the base of a different set of norms that govern attitudes toward what we call "academic integrity." I will start with the power of the written word, turn to the link between written and spoken words, and then point out the implications of deference, age, and authority. I will then explore the idea of collective responsibility and conclude by reviewing the effects of modernization and globalization on classroom behavior, academic integrity, conformity, rebellion, and dissent.

The Power of the Written and Spoken Word

From the earliest Chinese inscriptions on bronze and bamboo, more than 3,000 years ago, words were not merely descriptive; they were the means of discerning the will of a Heaven with the power to forecast the future, determine when to plant and when to reap, and decide whether to sue for peace or go to war. Heaven's blessings—and the largess of the emperors, generals, great poets, philosophers, and calligraphers—are still visible in carvings on stone stelae, on rocky promontories, and on temples high on mountain sides within Heaven's reach, on paintings, silk, and bamboo fans. To this day, monks, mediums, and fortune tellers rely on the written word to communicate with sages of the past, resolve conflicts, predict future events, and cure illnesses. Written characters testify not just to the skills of calligraphers, carvers and painters, and philosophers and poets: they reveal the strength of character that Heaven has conferred upon masters of the written word. This power has not waned. As can be seen in the Korean film *Spring, Summer, Fall, Winter ... Spring,* the written word carries weight (Baumgartner, Lee, & Kim, 2003). In the film, a deeply devoted Buddhist monk calms the soul of a murderer and relieves the anxieties of his captors by carving and then painting the words of the Lotus Sutra into the wood floor of his floating shrine.

By the end of the first century CE, the collected writings of the sages of the pre-imperial order formed a canon for the education of scholars and statesmen. That canon laid the foundations for the civil service examination system that held sway over education in China, Korea, and Japan right up until the beginning of the twentieth century. Rote learning lay at the system's base. Teaching was didactic and teacher-centered, not student-centered. Teachers and scholars were revered, and students expressed their reverence by regurgitating precisely, word for word, what their mentors, both living and dead, wrote and said. Mastery of the canon, for those who had access to education, started at a very early age with simplified versions of classic tomes that students learned to read and recite or, more accurately, chant in rhythmic unison. By the sixteenth century, mastery of the written word took the form of the "eight legged essay," a rigid, formulaic set of rules for classical commentaries embodied in the civil service examinations. This was a system that militated against innovation unless new visions could be couched in the reified language of the classical canon. Innovative ideas were absorbed into the canon.

When the civil service examination system came to end in 1908, it died as an institutional system, but because it was so firmly embedded in the consciousness of both Nationalist and Communist educators and ideologues, it continued to play a central role in the new, "modern" schools and universities. The establishment of Western-style missionary schools in the 1920s, with rare exceptions, did little to alter the didactic approach to teaching and learning by rote. Ideologues of the new "modern" political parties, Nationalist and Communist, held the highest degrees awarded by the civil service exam system, and drew their models of new "revolutionary" education from a potent mix of neo-Confucian ideas and practices as well as imported Western ideas and institutional structures, including Marxism (later, Leninism) and Russian and Japanese organizational models.

The demise of the imperial system left a vacuum to be filled by competing colonial powers, warlords, and remnants of the Qing Dynasty's secret service, along with new political factions, movements, and parties. By the late 1920s, the Nationalist and Communist parties had absorbed most of these contending groups, and new dogmas emerged to capture the power of both the written and spoken word. "The Three People's Principles," Sun Yat-sen's legacy to the Nationalist (Guomindang) Party, set the pace under Chiang Kai-shek for educational and ideological parroting, first in China and then, after 1947, in Taiwan. Filmmaker Zhang Yimou's romantic tale *The Road Home* (wodi fuqin muqin) gives us a glimpse of the teaching style of the times and the price of failure to toe the Party line in education (Zhao & Zhang, 1999). The writings of the Great Helmsman, Chairman Mao Zedong, and his leading general, Zhu De, were required reading for the cadres of the 8th Route Army. After the establishment of the People's Republic of China, Mao's "On Contradictions" served to set the tone for the ideological reform of China's millions throughout the 1950s, until Mao's collected works were encapsulated into the "Little Red Book" during the Cultural Revolution of 1966-1976.

Everyone was required to cite Mao word for word, which was not an easy matter since Mao's radio speeches were delivered in a heavily accented Hunanese dialect. In Taiwan, Chiang Kai-shek's speeches were similarly accented in his Zhejiang voice. Footnotes were irrelevant. In post-liberation China, few dared take issue with the constant barrage of incantations from the works of Chairman Mao. They became instruments of class warfare serving to isolate and punish those targeted as "traitors," "landlords," "rightists," "counter-revolutionaries," and later "freaks," "snakes," and "monsters" (niu, gui, she, shen) in the all-embracing cauldron that was the Great Proletarian Cultural Revolution. Some sense of the terror that these political campaigns unleashed can be gleaned in films. Director Tian Zhuang Zhuang's *The Blue Kite* follows the story of a single family in one village as they are subjected to the succession of political campaigns, starting with the Anti-Rightist Campaign of 1958 through the Great Leap Forward and the Cultural Revolution (Cheng, Luo, & Tian, 1993).

Learning to read between the lines of propaganda, cultivating silence, launching attacks to defray attacks, and mastering the power of the written and spoken word became defensive strategies in those trying times. This was not limited to China and Taiwan. In Korea, following the end of the Korean War, and through the years of military rule and the suppression of student protests, these same lessons applied. The least indication of temerity, rebellion, or insincerity in self-criticism and class struggle could be disastrous, not just for oneself but for entire families, clans, and communities. Intellectuals were particularly vulnerable. While the trials and tribulations of target groups in China were duplicated in the experiences of the Taiwanese in Taiwan, a substantial number of Taiwanese intellectuals escaped by studying at Japanese and U.S. institutions of higher education. In the relative safety of American and Japanese universities in the 1960s and 70s, this group laid the foundations of the Taiwan independence movement.

Defiance, Deviance, and the Decline of the Power of the Written and Spoken Word and Retreat from the Collective

The succession of campaigns and their devastating impact meant that many intellectuals learned not only to read between the lines of documents, orders, notices, and speeches, but also to cheat the system that so oppressed them. They used a variety of means to do so, some excruciatingly difficult. Forging confessions and self-criticisms, feigning cooperation with their oppressors, and in not a few cases, turning friends and family over to Public Security were among those strategies (Greenblatt, 1977). Silence in the face of disaster, in order to protect parents, spouses, and children, fractured many families, and it is only in the last two decades that the silence has been broken. In the last stages of the Cultural Revolution, young Red Guard college students broke into the Public Security files to discover their own political dossiers collected over their school years. They destroyed the files, but not before publishing them in Red Guard newspapers. In those files lay the evidence of the corrupt use of the power of the written and spoken word in the manufacture and dissemination of propaganda. The campaign against the "Four Olds" that marked the beginning of the Cultural Revolution struck a blow against norms of deference to age and authority, and the rebellion seeped into the social and cultural fabric in China, as it did in the rise of the Taiwan independence movement. In the case of Taiwan, student rebellion first simmered and then boiled over among Taiwanese students studying in the United States, free as they were from at least some of the sources of oppression.

I saw the signs of that rebellion in 1983 when I contracted with a Hong Kong agency to recruit American doctors to attend medical conferences in Tianjin at the No.1 Tianjin Hospital. At one point, as senior physicians and hospital administrators droned on from the podium, I overheard a group of young medical students sitting behind me. Their acid comments interrupted the conference proceedings: "old Party hack, we've listened to you for years, and you still have nothing to say" was one of the less acerbic comments made by the chorus of voices around me. This was not the first round in the torrent of rebellion against authority. Students and faculty denounced the new "eight legged essays," the pedagogy of rote learning, and the college entrance examination system in the "100 Flowers" campaign of 1957-1958. They were rudely suppressed and subjected to "reform" at the time. The chorus of dissent laid the foundations for the protest at Tiananmen in 1989 (Spence, 2003). In Taiwan, the democracy movement laid the groundwork for the Kaohsiung Incident of 1979, when young dissidents celebrated the anniversary of the Universal Declaration of Human Rights and were charged with sedition. While the dissent among students was met with force, reform of the educational system and relaxation of ideological constraints followed the Tiananmen massacre in China and the death of Chiang Kai-shek in Taiwan.

Normalization of relations between China and the United States paved the way for Chinese students to enter U.S. colleges and universities. Until the early 1980s, students from Taiwan were the largest segment of the Asian student population on American campuses. Networks of English-language training institutions helped to improve performance on TOEFL tests in Korea, China, and Taiwan. By the late 1990s, the first sizeable contingents of graduates returned to their home countries to fill teaching posts in the most eminent of their nation's educational institutions. They were the first generation of new educators steeped in American-style, student-centered pedagogy. In the years since the late 1990s, their numbers have grown. Their influence is, however, limited because they are young, their numbers are still relatively small, and the regimes they serve have not, as of this date, made peace with the past. In the meantime, as rapid economic growth increases disposable incomes in Asia, more and more students of ever-increasing diversity have access to higher education at home and abroad. We have more women and minorities among our international students than ever before.

Many of those students, but certainly not all, are poorly prepared for entry into the U.S. system, either in terms of English language preparation or in terms of adjustment to U.S educational norms. This is particularly pertinent with respect to students coming from regions beyond the major cities and well-funded institutions of China's east coast, beyond the most prominent universities in Korea, and in Taiwan. Students from the hinterlands are more likely to come from educational institutions that are teacher-centered, not learner-centered. They are more likely to trace descent from families that observe traditional and collective norms and to come from minority backgrounds (the Hui, Miao, Manchu, Uighur, and Tibetans in China; aboriginals and rural Taiwanese in Taiwan; North Koreans and Chinese in Korea). That scenario changes as modernization and globalization extend further into less developed and less advantaged regions of any given country. At the same time, these are the students who will ultimately displace an older generation of faculty. They are driven to succeed by parents whose sole hope, after so many disappointments, rests on the shoulders of their children—or, where the one-child policy holds sway, their one and only child. That pressure to succeed helps to account for China's and South Korea's rapid economic growth. But growing up in a pressure cooker is not particularly conducive to norms of academic integrity or individual health and wellness. Children who lose "face," another traditional concept that has survived modernization and globalization, do so not just for themselves, but for their families, their communities, and their home countries (Greenblatt, 1979). With so high a price for failure, silence, self-starvation, isolation, and cheating are all among the unhappy options from which students sometimes choose at the risk of being labeled devious and unwelcome "aliens."

Given the rapid pace of modernization and change, it is no longer a simple ecological formula that determines where traditionalist and modern values are situated. Children growing up in a traditional family and attending traditional schools may live right around the corner from modern families with children who attend modern schools.

The fact that "modern" pedagogy and English language training is now in the offing throughout Asia does nothing to ensure that students learn about American academic norms and expectations.

The fact that "modern" pedagogy and English language training is now in the offing throughout Asia does nothing to ensure that students learn about American academic norms and expectations. Nor do course syllabi with instructions on academic integrity assure compliance. We know that well enough from the behavior of American students.

Case Studies in Normative Maladaptation and Misinterpretation

I have tried to make the case that written and spoken words are filtered through language, culture, and experience. International students no longer express surprise when they see the sign outside the door of our office that says "No Standing," but there was a time, not so long ago, when the words on the sign denoted American obsession with legal norms. What other society prohibits individuals from standing on the sidewalk? Two more examples will suffice to make this point about cultural and linguistic filters.

One Saturday morning, a Chinese student was busy setting up the fax machine for a message to his parents. The instructions were pasted on the wall above the fax machine. While he was focusing on this task, the dean walked in, turned to the student and said, "You can't do that!" The student, looking directly at the instructions on the wall, replied "Yes, I can." After a moment's pause the dean said, "You'll pay for that!" to which the student replied, "Yes, I will," and the dean left the room. By the end of the following week, the student received a letter from the dean accusing him of having violated university rules that prohibited student use of the departmental fax machine. The dean also accused the student of being "hostile." In his replies to the dean the student had, of course, been referring to his ability to understand the instructions on the use of the fax. He had always paid the departmental secretary for phone calls home from the departmental office, and he had intended to do the same on this occasion. As for being "hostile," the student was concentrating intently on his task (brows furrowed, eyes focused straight ahead, jaw clenched). Having been an interpreter for delegations from China over a long period of time, I am aware of American hosts' misreading of Chinese faces. "Skip," they would say, "I don't think they like what I am saying," interpreting intense concentration as a sign of distaste or disagreement.

This is not mere happenstance. Homeland Security's profile of the facial expression of "angry" men, used for training airport security personnel to spot potential terrorists, commits the same error confounding concentration and hostility. A student's silence when classroom discussions and opinions are called for is often confounded with inability to think out loud, absorb concepts, or take the initiative, when deference to faculty is, in fact, the reason for failure to "speak up" in class and express his or her own opinions. A group of students in an engineering class, all of whom were Asian, were charged with violating academic integrity. The instructions on the syllabus made it clear, so the professor thought, that the work submitted for grades had to be one's own. These students shared notes and discussed their lab procedures and findings with one another. Appalled by the charges filed against them, they launched a counterattack on the Internet until their professor discovered the online rebellion and joined the fray. Chaos ensued. Most of the students were eventually given the opportunity to repeat the course. The incident's lasting feature, however, was an unresolved conflict pitting collectivist and collaborative notions of moral and ethical responsibility against individualist, competitive norms and values.

Mediating Cultural Differences: Five Suggestions Toward a Sustainable Approach to Academic Integrity

1. If "know thyself" was once central to classical Western pedagogy, knowing the other and oneself through the other is the sine qua non of the extraordinarily dangerous world we now inhabit. There is no substitute for shared, thoughtful inquiry into the backgrounds of both domestic and international students,

assuming that "sharing" is spontaneous, voluntary, and reciprocal. Of course, this approach assumes that all parties to the interaction that ensues are sufficiently articulate to be heard, and that partners to the interaction are capable of listening. Listening gets minimal attention in the discourse about language skills. We, who often demand that foreigners speak English "just as we do," have the skills to understand sentences spoken by foreigners with erroneous tense, inappropriate prepositions, missing articles, and what we perceive as awkward phrasing. The rewards of good listening are often the first tentative steps toward real and lasting relationships that make learning of any kind, including the learning of academic norms, much easier.

2. Orientation programs that prepare students for entry into the U.S. academic normative order are all too frequently classes in the rules of proper citation presented in true didactic style and accompanied by handouts that supplement the volumes of documentary material that accompany every other facet of an orientation program. They are lost in the pile of accumulated paper. Academic integrity is too important a topic to rest on didactic grounds. It should be separated from general orientation, so that time is allocated to a survey of student experiences, and their understandings of plagiarism, competition, and collaboration, in order to arrive at a consensus to which the students themselves have contributed.

3. Calling upon on the aid and support of international student associations on campus is a must. At Syracuse University, the Chinese Students and Scholars Association (CSSA), the Korean Students Association (KSA), and the Taiwan Students Association (TSA) have all run their own orientation sessions and provided housing to incoming students. They all organize cultural events, and in the case of CSSA run seminars on U.S.-China diplomatic, trade, and cultural relations. All three have, at one time or another, produced handbooks and run workshops for their constituents. As sources of support for adaptation to U.S. academic culture, these groups and others like them are indispensable. At the very least, they should be honored for the roles they play and acknowledged as cultural mediators. That happens all too rarely.

4. Imparting norms of academic integrity cannot be left to written instructions on syllabi. Bereft of context, discussion, and validation, these norms are little more than street signs that say "No Standing." Faculty, staff, and students need to understand that being in America, doing it the way we do, subject to our norms, is rarely reversible (Tucker, 2003; Shei, 2005). Few Americans would be able to make sense out of similar "instructions" in Chinese or Korean, much less be able to read between the lines of the text to find out how those instructions are actually carried out in the face of the cultural filters through which they take on meaning (Saltmarsh, 2005).[1] That enterprise requires acknowledgement of the diverse experiences our international students

bring to the tasks they are asked to perform, so that consensus reigns and adaptation to a different normative order is assured (Greenblatt, 2005). Lopsided, one-way expectations do little to sustain academic integrity.

5. Offices of International Services can and should play an important role in the creation of the kind of consensus I am recommending here. Such centers are staffed with professionals who have the experience and the linguistic and listening skills to "hear" cultural and linguistic differences, including accented or ungrammatical English. And in many cases they have the background and experience to assess the role of the sociocultural filters used in adapting to American educational norms—or, if they don't, they know where to find the necessary expertise among students, staff, faculty, and members of the on- and off-campus communities (Smithee, Greenblatt, & Eland 2004).

Notes

1. Saltmarsh takes a broader and very critical stance, and applies a deconstructionist analytical framework linking profit-making capitalist educational institutions and patent racism when international students, particularly Asian students, are identified as the perpetrators of plagiarism. I do not share that view. In my view, ignorance of international diversity plays a greater role than racism in the charge of plagiarism against Asian students.

Works Cited

Baumgartner, K. (Producer), Lee, S. (Producer), & Kim, K. (Director). (2003). *Spring, summer, fall, winter... spring* [Motion picture]. South Korea: Korea Pictures.

Cheng, Y. (Line Producer), Luo, G. (Line Producer), & Tian, Z. Z. (Director). (1993). *The blue kite* (lan fengzheng) [Motion Picture]. China: Beijing Film Studio.

Greenblatt, S. L. (1977). Campaigns and the manufacture of deviance. In A. A. Wilson & R. W. Wilson (Eds.), *Deviance and social control in the People's Republic of China* (pp. 82-120). New York: Praeger.

Greenblatt, S. L. (1979, May-June). Chinese fortune-telling in action. *The Humanist, 39*(3), 21-28.

Greenblatt, S. L. (2005). International students and diversity in American higher education: Implications for internationalization. *International Journal of Diversity in Organisations, Communities and Nations, 5*(2), 163-1672.

Saltmarsh, S. (2005). 'White pages' in the academy: Plagiarism, consumption, and racist rationalities [Electronic version]. *International Journal for Educational Integrity* 1(1), n.p.

Shei, C. (2005). Plagiarism, Chinese learners and Western convention. *Taiwan Journal of TESOL*, 2(1), 97-113.

Smithee, M., Greenblatt, S. L., & Eland, A. (2004). *U.S. classroom culture.* Washington, DC: NAFSA, Association of International Educators.

Spence, J. (2003). *The search for modern China.* New York: New York Times Books.

Tucker, D. L. (2003). *Understanding learning styles and study strategies of Korean students in American colleges and universities: A research study with recommendations for faculty and academic advisors.* (ERIC Document Reproduction Service No. ED 478 616)

Zhao, Y. (Producer), & Zhang, Y. (Director). (1999). *The road home* (wodi fuqin muqin) [Motion picture]. China: Columbia Pictures Film Production Asia.

IV
INTEGRITY IN ASSESSMENT
STRATEGIES FOR TAS

TEACHING ASSISTANTS ARE VITAL to both undergraduates and faculty—and as such they commonly find themselves overworked in both capacities, under-prepared in one or both, and caught in the dexterity-demanding position of being asked to play catch-up *and* juggle numerous competing demands. In addition to being graduate students and researchers, TAs often take on the role of the instructor of record in courses, but do not have the privileges that faculty have. Much of what a TA knows about her work comes through "on-the-job" training.

A number of aspects of academic integrity are specific to teaching assistants. First, a teaching assistantship is, in a sense, an "entry level" academic position. The mechanisms of teaching are relatively new to TAs, many of whom have a lot of experience being a student but are new to being on the other side of the podium. Second, a TA's experience as a student may serve as an excellent resource for understanding the undergraduate perspective—or it may not. There might be a good number of years between a TA and his students, the TA may be from another culture, or the TA just may have been a different kind of student than the ones he has in his class. In any of these cases, the TA will find himself out of touch with the spectrum of student habits and attitudes—and so be susceptible to surprise. Third, a TA is often in a unique situation, having some authority but not complete control of the planning and implementation of the course. This means negotiating multiple agendas, teaching or reviewing material she did not select and may not be very familiar with, and often deferring to an instructional style that she may not share. Fourth, the TA is most often a busy graduate student herself who is expected to prioritize her own research yet devote considerable time to the class she is TAing for. Assessing students—their conduct, their learning, their participation, their mastery of material, and their honesty or *dishonesty* in producing and submitting work often falls to TAs, as they oversee labs and sections, proctor exams, and grade tests, among other tasks. This section is targeted at reducing the time spent in learning the ropes, preventing conflict, and helping the TA handle conflicts and other unexpected situations when they inevitably arise.

Kevin Yee and Patricia MacKown, authors from the University of Central Florida, offer an extensive list of methods used by students to cheat on exams in large lecture courses. The list is useful beyond its immediate application of detecting or preventing certain behaviors: it can be used to deflect some of the surprise (and appreciation for student ingenuity!) that may blind a TA in the moment and keep him from dealing with the behavior. In lieu of the ideal proctoring situation, this list stands as a reminder of the effort of students to challenge the constraints of their environments to achieve their own goals, and includes 37 tactics used by students to bring outside information into a testing environment to impede genuine assessment. Sarah Bolton offers a comprehensive guide to academic integrity for the large lecture class, focusing her chapter on climate and preventive pedagogy. From her experience in a General Chemistry course, Bolton speaks to the simultaneous forces of anonymity and competition that contribute to the character of large classes and create particular concerns for their teachers. Brian Udermann and Karrie Lamers extend Bolton's work by giving ten tips for bringing out the best in a large lecture class. These techniques have wider applications, and TAs of any size class may find these tips helpful in building a productive classroom culture.

Michael Smithee offers reflections about a different type of assessment TAs are frequently asked to undertake: that of assessing international students' cultural awareness and understanding of American university expectations so as to distinguish between mistakes, misunderstandings, and deliberately inappropriate academic behaviors. As Smithee makes clear, an important part of this skill involves examining and coming to understand the way one's own culture influences one's understandings and expectations. Danielle Schuehler's chapter on the "dreaded" lab report has the most to say to a hard-science audience anxious about made-up data and textbook answers. But for readers who have not been near a beaker since high school, it gives an illuminating look at the pressures and products of scientific investigation. Being a TA means something different to each discipline, and thus the circumstances wherein assessing students can raise issues of integrity have a wide range. A commonly referenced issue is plagiarism. This is perhaps a product of the high anxiety surrounding changes in electronic culture and the disparity in tech savvyness between many students and their instructors. In her timely evaluation of electronic plagiarism detection systems, Tyra Twomey gives insight into this high-profile yet controversial software. She shares research that exposes its weaknesses as a surveillance tool but also highlights its strengths for teaching citation styles.

Experience is a wonderful teacher, and this section will not rob you as a TA of this most excellent (if humbling) instructor! If you are a TA, we hope that this section gives you valuable information in an accessible format. If you are a lead teacher, we hope that you take something away that you can apply to the courses you teach (and, potentially, the TAs you work with). In either case, trust your instincts and know your school's policy. This will instill the confidence you need to confront academic integrity violations and give you your own ideas for communicating effectively with your students, so that you understand each others' positions and expectations.

Ten Strategies to Encourage Academic Integrity in Large Lecture Classes

Brian Udermann and Karrie Lamers

Introduction

Academic integrity has been and continues to be a lively topic of discussion on most college and university campuses. Many articles and books have been written about cheating and have explored such topics as why students cheat, how students cheat, ways to discourage cheating, and faculty and student attitudes towards cheating. Both students and faculty must take steps and assume some responsibility if the current culture regarding academic integrity in higher education is to change. This chapter presents ten strategies that can be used in large lecture courses (the authors consistently teach sections that have enrollments between 400 and 500 students). Some of the strategies discussed in the chapter are specific to large lecture courses, but many of the strategies would be appropriate to use in courses with smaller enrollments as well.

1. Promote your school's honor code.

Many faculty members do not even realize that their college or university has an honor code, and many who do fail to discuss and promote it with their students. A university's honor code or policy on academic integrity should be reviewed often and shared with students on a continual basis. It has been our experience that many students in our large lecture courses have never seen information on academic integrity on a syllabus or had open discussions on cheating in the classroom. If more faculty members would have open and frank discussions about integrity with their students, the overall attitude regarding cheating would likely start to change.

2. Respond to cheating in your class.

Taking action against a student cheating in your class is not a pleasant experience. Some faculty overlook cheating simply because they do not want the added stress in their life, and it can also become very time consuming (meetings with the student and school officials, written reports of the incident in question,

If more faculty members would have open and frank discussions about integrity with their students, the overall attitude regarding cheating would likely start to change.

hearings, etc.). One of the authors recalls the first time he confronted a student cheating in a class he was teaching as a graduate student. The student became very angry and upset, said there was no proof that any cheating had occurred, and threatened to file a complaint with the university. Understandably, this resulted in a great deal of stress. Ironically, it was a stress management course that was being taught! Luckily, the department chair-

person was extremely supportive, the complaint was never filed, and the student received a zero on the exam. One thing we are not shy about doing when giving exams in our large lecture courses is to respond quickly when we think someone may be cheating. If we find a student whose eyes appear to be wandering a bit, we require the student to move to a different section of the classroom, often from the back to the front. Shortly after moving the student, we usually make an announcement to the class and say something to the effect of "please keep your eyes on your own exam" or "please do your own work." This sends a strong message—students are often a bit shocked to see this take place—to the other 400 or 500 students in the auditorium that cheating will not be tolerated. Over the course of the past few years, we have done this with dozens of students and not once has it resulted in a student complaint.

3. Individualize papers and assignments to the class if possible.

One strategy faculty can use to discourage cheating in large lectures is to individualize assignments and papers to their respective courses. For example, we recently created a civic engagement assignment for our large health and wellness course, in which students had to research and determine what avenues or resources were locally available to them to be physically active (e.g., bike trails, walking paths). For this assignment, students also had to list five potential avenues or resources for physical activity that were not available in their community and determine whom they would need to contact to see if the addition of such a resource would be feasible. This was a great assignment in that it encouraged critical thinking and invited community involvement. It was also a unique assignment, one that could not be completed through any means other than conducting the necessary research.

Some faculty who teach large lectures will also frequently change assignments in order to discourage cheating. This makes it harder for students to use and turn in assignments from previous semesters. Also, an additional strategy that can be used if students write papers in your course is to make the topic more narrow or specific. So, instead of having students write a general paper on eating disorders, you could have them focus on one very specific component of the topic.

4. Give clear expectations for assignments and other course work required of students.

We have noticed that students are more confident and more likely to do their own work when they receive clear directions and expectations for assignments, papers, lab reports, class projects, etc. Sometimes it can feel like we are over-communicating with our students and that we are holding their hands a bit too much, but clarity and communication are especially important in large lecture courses. If you teach a course of 500 students, you probably do not take attendance, and it is reasonable to assume that 50 to 100 students will miss any given lecture. Our assignments are all described in a lab manual that we give students.; they are also posted on the course management tool we use for the class. The assignments are always discussed in class, and e-mails are often sent regarding assignments to remind students of due dates and clarify details. The tremendous focus on group work in colleges and universities today can sometimes become problematic for students. Sometimes student collaboration becomes the norm, and students might not know when they are expected to do their own work or work in teams. Clear descriptions and expectations can certainly help clarify this.

5. Encourage student responsibility.

Faculty are in the ideal position to discuss academic integrity with their students, and more importantly to encourage and challenge students to change the culture surrounding cheating. One of the strongest motivators students have for avoiding cheating is sensing or experiencing strong peer disapproval. It is our responsibility as educators to stir up this desire in students to do what is right. That might include emphasizing to students that they are expected to do their own work or reporting other students who they know are cheating. Much has been written about the "millennial student." Some believe the students we have in class today are more responsible, more open to our influence, and more concerned with doing what is right. Within our large lecture course, we often have discussions with students about how harmful cheating can be and how much of an influence it could have on them once they graduate and get a job. Individuals who consistently cheat can certainly lack skills such as critical thinking and the ability to solve problems—both extremely helpful skills to have when entering the job market. The exciting thing about having such discussions in large lecture courses is having the potential to influence such a large number of students. Some faculty may mistakenly think that because they teach a large lecture course, students do not really listen to, care about, or pay attention to what they say. We have found just the opposite to be true. If you truly care for your students and show you are passionate about a topic, even academic integrity, you will impact students!

6. Get to know as many students as possible.

This may seem like a strange strategy for promoting academic integrity in your large lecture course, but we believe that learning the names of as many students as possible and getting to know your students will help deter cheating in your class. A few ways you can do this are by asking for students' names when you call on them to answer questions, paying close attention to their names when you hand back assignments or exams, and arriving to class five to ten minutes early to interact with your students. We teach in a very large auditorium and try to select different sections of the classroom in which to interact with students before class; that way we are meeting and interacting with a wide variety of students. It really is amazing, even in a class of 500, how many students we can get to know with a little bit of effort. Before a lecture one morning, one of the authors met a young lady sitting in the auditorium waiting for class and learned that she was a high-level power lifter. Two and a half weeks later, the topic of the day was resistance training and the importance of proper breathing. The young power lifter, who had just returned from overseas and had won a power lifting world championship, was more than happy to share her expertise on the topic. That interaction might not have occurred if the faculty member had not made an effort to get to know students. If students get the impression that you care about them and you are genuinely concerned about them learning the course material, we believe they will be less likely to cheat in class.

7. Separate students during exams, when space permits.

Nearly every seat in our auditorium is full during our exams. However, after approximately two-thirds of the students have finished with the exam, we require students to move so as to have at least one empty seat between them. Also, after approximately 75 or 80 percent of students have taken the exam, we require students to move into one section of the auditorium as they complete their exam. Students who are very prepared to take the exam often complete it in less time than individuals who are not, or individuals who are attempting to cheat. Two additional strategies for deterring exam cheating are to encourage students to keep answer sheets covered as much as possible and to check IDs when students turn in their exams, making sure the name on the exam matches the name on the ID.

8. Have adequate proctors to help with exams.

When giving an exam to over 500 students, it is extremely important to ensure that there are enough proctors present. At a minimum, there are eight proctors present at each exam we give. Not only are these individuals responsible for monitoring the students while they are taking the exam, but the proctors can also hand out answer sheets as students enter the room and distribute tests to a specified section of the room. This can significantly reduce the amount of time spent on exam set-up. It is then the responsibility of the proctor to watch over the particular section for any unusual behavior. It is beneficial to put more than one proctor in the larger sections if numbers allow. The mere presence of the proctors seems to deter students from engaging in unethical behavior, making the job of the proctor relatively simple. The proctors should walk around the section designated to them rather than being stationary, as this enhances their presence. Another role the proctors play is collecting the exams. Typically, two versions of the exam are given, and these need to be collected separately. At a minimum, proctors check the Scantron forms to make sure the student has put the right version of the exam down and also included her student ID number.

9. Have multiple versions of exams.

As previously mentioned, we use multiple versions of exams when we give tests. As with the presence of the proctors, the mere awareness of the multiple exams seems to deter students from cheating. To keep the tests the same for every student taking the exam, the same questions are used on each test—they are just arranged in a different order. Many faculty develop a large bank of test questions and periodically rotate the questions on the exams. We always administer exams in at least two different colors. This helps the proctors who distribute the exams make sure students are not sitting next to someone with the same version of the test. If at all possible, we would recommend using exam formats other than multiple choice (e.g., short answer, essay). This may only be possible if adequate teaching assistants or graduate assistants are assigned to the class to help with grading.

10. Engage your students and be enthusiastic.

It is time that we educators also consider why students cheat and possibly accept some of the responsibility ourselves. While many students cheat due to the pressures to succeed and obtain higher grades, they are just as likely to cheat when assignments are boring as when they are difficult. We believe that many students cheat because they are not engaged in their classrooms. They are not being motivated to learn, and they are not being inspired by faculty members who are enthusiastic about the content they are teaching. This can be especially problematic in large lecture courses, for obvious reasons. Some faculty members do an excellent job when it comes to engaging students and motivating them to learn, but the sad reality is that many do not. Many students sit in large lectures and are bored, or apathetic, or fall asleep. They are simply not stimulated by the course content or the individual delivering the material. It certainly can be challenging to prepare a course that encourages frequent student engagement, and some educators may not be comfortable teaching extremely large lecture courses. These are important factors to consider and can impact academic integrity. It is beyond the scope of this chapter to discuss strategies that can be used to engage students in large lecture courses; however, many articles and even some books have been written on the topic. Anecdotally, we can tell you that as we have tried to engage and stimulate students in our large lecture courses over the past few years, the amount of cheating we have encountered has decreased.

While many students cheat due to the pressures to succeed and obtain higher grades, they are just as likely to cheat when assignments are boring as when they are difficult.

Conclusion

In this chapter we have presented a variety of strategies faculty can utilize to encourage academic integrity in large lecture courses. We believe that it is possible to have an impact on the amount of cheating that occurs on college and university campuses, but this will certainly take some effort on the part of both students and faculty. We believe that if we as faculty encourage student responsibility, have open and frank discussions about cheating, are more willing to respond when students cheat, and focus on ways to engage students and improve our teaching, the current culture surrounding cheating will start to change.

Temptations in the Large Lecture Class
Concrete Measures to Help Students Practice Academic Integrity[1]

Sarah L. Bolton

IN ORDER TO DEVELOP an academic integrity policy for a large class, it is necessary to know the type of student that will be taking the course. The students in General Chemistry, the course with which I have experience teaching a large lecture class, are characteristically very grade-driven because most will be applying to obtain a higher level of education after college. In other words, a good number of students feel it necessary to get an A in the class due to the standards set by medical, dental, veterinary, and graduate schools. General Chemistry often gets a reputation for "weeding out" students; a poor grade in this course could critically affect a student's future. This cutthroat mentality may make a student desperate to get the best grade possible, at any cost. "At any cost" usually involves some all-nighters and the lack of a social life; however, some students will be tempted to resort to academic dishonesty as a means to succeed.

General Chemistry classes at Syracuse University typically enroll 160-220 students with a wide variety of scientific backgrounds. It is a mandatory course for science and engineering majors. The diverse scientific experience of the students often makes it difficult for a professor to gauge how thoroughly to teach and test—being too general can bore the more advanced students, while too much specificity could discourage the weaker ones. Most students taking introductory level science courses have taken high school chemistry within the past year, but some find that they need to work much harder in college than they did in high school to be in the top of the class. One of the most common complaints after the first exam is from students who were in the top of the class in high school but are now getting average or even below average grades. Such a grade is disappointing to the student, but also carries with it the burden that it must be explained to parents and mentors with high expectations. A student

117

under such pressure may go to great and troubling lengths to get a higher grade in his or her required general science classes.

Cheating on an exam is typically preceded by panic. This panic results from the fear of failure, which can lead even the most habitually honest students to resort to unethical behavior. Unfortunately, in a large classroom setting such as in General Chemistry, this fear is often accompanied by circumstances that are optimal for cheating—tests taken in a large, cramped room with too few proctors and plenty of distractions. It is at that point when a casual or even a forceful reminder is valuable to help the student make the best decision with regard to maintaining academic integrity.

The strategies described below are not intended to scare students, but should reinforce the importance of upholding the academic integrity policy. I have not personally performed any scientific studies or surveys to support the strategies below; all are based on my personal experience and are simply suggestions that have prevented the professors and proctors that I have worked with from having to deal with a situation involving a breach of the academic integrity policy. (The chart found at the end of the chapter gives a summarized outline of each suggestion, as well as indications of when during the semester to implement each strategy.)

The backbone of any academic integrity policy in a particular class is the syllabus. A well-written syllabus should prevent any confusion about that class's policy. Often, professors or teaching assistants assume (or hope) that the students will carefully read the entire syllabus. This is not usually the case. For this reason, although it may take extra time, the academic integrity policy should be reviewed by the professor on the first day of class. Having the students sign a sheet stating the policy and the student's agreement to honor it is an excellent way to bring attention to the subject. (Students who add the class after the policy has been explained should sign the agreement prior to the first graded assignment or exam.) Most people will not provide their signature unless they read a document carefully.

Having the students sign a sheet stating the policy and the student's agreement to honor it is an excellent way to bring attention to the subject. Most people will not provide their signature unless they read a document carefully.

At this point, the student will hopefully see the importance of this policy and respect the efforts made to uphold it throughout the semester. This also gives proof that the student knew the policy prior to any testing situation, if a case of dishonesty should arise.

In a large class, it is difficult if not impossible for the professor or teaching assistants to be acquainted with every student by name and face. Teaching assistants often get to know the students better as a result of having them in small recitation or lab sections (approximately 30 students per section); however, the TAs are generally not present during lectures. Taking attendance by calling out each name can often be time-consuming and is unreliable. Passing around an attendance sheet is a simple way for students to prove they attend class on a regular basis. This presents a situation that some students do not recognize as a matter of academic dishonesty. Forging a signature for a classmate is a temptation that can easily be deterred. It should be clearly written and stated that the signature on the attendance sheet will be compared to the one given on the first day of class. If there is a punishment for missing class, students are more likely to forge another's signature, with the mindset that they are "saving" a friend. If, instead, having excellent attendance carries a reward, the student will be less inclined to break the rules.

As the semester rolls on, students often forget which reading assignments to finish for a particular lecture and when homework is due; this also means that the academic integrity section of the syllabus is becoming hazy. Requiring a signature on every examination paper and attendance sheet should compel the students to remember the promise they made on the first day of class. This again provides confirmation of the understanding of the academic integrity policy.

In large classroom settings it is sometimes hard to provide a suitable testing environment. Spreading students out—a seat and a row apart, for example—drastically decreases the urge to cheat, simply by making the act more difficult. Copying from a neighbor becomes physically more challenging if that neighbor is one or more seats away. In steep lecture halls, seating students directly behind each other forces a cheater to make additional lateral movements to be successful. Increased movement or agitation is generally a telltale sign of unethical behavior. Available space in the lecture hall is generally the restricting factor limiting the dispersal of students; this may mean using two or more testing rooms. Generally, the rooms need to be scheduled months in advance, so planning ahead is essential. This allows for flexibility in seating arrangements. If multiple rooms are used, a method of communication needs to be available between testing rooms, by either telephone or a messenger—if there is a mistake found on the examination forms or an announcement needs to be made, every testing room needs to be informed.

General Chemistry professors will occasionally make up different versions of an exam; this will make it extremely hard for a student to copy off a neighbor because their questions are different or at least in a different order. The use of this strategy may well seem like extra work to some professors, and therefore is not consistently exercised; however, it is one of the most reliable ways to prevent cheating on multiple-choice exams. (Even the threat of different versions will discourage cheating, and will not make for any additional grading.)

The advancement of technology also gives rise to new technological approaches to cheating. Electronic calculators, which used to be mathematical tools, have now become miniature storage devices. Memorization has essentially become obsolete. This is fine, unless the subject being tested requires the students to memorize specific equations, facts, or figures. In other words, a calculator can store everything a student needs to pass an exam; however, in the long run it would benefit the student more if he or she actually learned the material rather than simply copying it from a calculator. A simple scientific calculator, which can perform logarithm functions, is necessary for General Chemistry. However, most students require a more advanced calculator for their upper level math and science courses, and these can be misused to store pro-hibited information. Calculator checks during an exam have become important; two methods that show good results are randomly checking about 15% of the calculators, and simply deleting all RAM memory of every calculator that comes through the door. (The commands for deleting the RAM are different for each model of calculator, but most have a "Mem" function button; once this is activated, simply follow the commands that will lead to the RAM deletion. If this fails, typically removing the batteries for a few minutes should work.) These precautions may seem time-consuming, but preventing cheating is the best way to avoid a difficult situation. Storing unauthorized data in a calculator constitutes cheating, and the penalty should reflect that. Other personal belongings that can store data should not be allowed into the testing area. Devices such as a walkman, MP3 player, or cell phone are not essential and should be prohibited or at least required to be turned off and collected in a separate part of the testing room. An announcement should be made reminding students to turn off any electronics; this will prevent a disruption later during the exam.

Cheating is not restricted to the electronic variety; old-fashioned dishonesty is still a tempting option. To reduce this form of cheating, all books and loose papers need to be removed from the testing area. A little creativity can turn otherwise harmless items into possible cheating tools. Possessions such as food containers, beverages, and even caps can be turned into portable data storage. Calculator cases should also be checked, as they can be a compartment for cheat sheets. Personal belongings, such as purses, bags, and coats, need to be placed out of reach, to avoid being a distraction. Any student requests to bring nonessential items to the exam (such as tissues, cough drops, or a clock) need to be approved prior to the exam, and the professor should make the decision concerning what to allow.

Providing students with plenty of supplemental material, such as tables, charts, or numerical constants not requiring memorization, during a test will reduce the temptation for students to smuggle in their own. In General Chemistry, each student is given a new periodic table for every exam; this prevents people from bringing in their personal copy that may have notes or hints written on it (and keeps students from being tempted to write lists of atomic numbers on their arms!). Rules about what is allowed during an exam need to be clearly explained to students and proctors prior to the exam date. Making it extremely clear what specific details or facts need to be memorized and what, if any, additional material is acceptable will reduce the anxiety associated with cramming for an exam.

Providing supplemental material and making it extremely clear what specific details or facts need to be memorized and what, if any, additional material is acceptable will reduce the anxiety associated with cramming for an exam.

For instance, before the final exam I inform students that the speed of light needs to be memorized, but the ideal gas constant, along with its units, is given. This specification also functions as a hint of what should be focused on while studying—i.e., if the speed of light needs to be memorized, it will most likely need to be used to solve a problem.

A simple proctoring technique that can be applied to prevent academic dishonesty is "active proctoring." Active proctoring involves virtually constant movement by the proctors. Proctors should shift positions and spread out throughout the testing space. Using this technique, a small number of proctors can cover much more space and notice suspicious behavior without difficulty. Active proctoring promotes academic honesty and concurrently allows proctors to be available to answer questions in far corners of the room. This encourages more reserved students, who would be unlikely to draw attention to themselves across a large room, to ask questions that would clarify otherwise confusing language or instructions. Ideally, the student-to-proctor ratio should be at most 25:1. Proctors need to be recruited early in the semester and given a schedule of the dates and times they will be needed.

If a proctor suspects that dishonest behavior may be occurring, a simple announcement such as, "We have reason to believe someone may be cheating; please keep your eyes on your own paper," is often an effective deterrent. Even if there is no suspicious activity, this statement, or a variation, is useful to discourage a potential cheater who is thinking about being dishonest but has not yet crossed that line.

A final reminder of the importance of honesty is the requirement that each student must show photo identification before handing in the exam. A rare but serious form of cheating involves a student "stand in," in which a more qualified person takes the exam. Announcing prior to the test that students' IDs will be examined when the student turns in the exam provides a substantial deterrent for this severe form of academic dishonesty. Also, requiring that each person write his or her student ID number on the examination paper will help further verify his or her identity. To some students, this strategy may seem slightly invasive; it is a good idea to remind them that this precaution is simply another method to provide the most honest testing environment possible. Proctors should take the ID process seriously and check the name and picture of the student; this is not meant to intimidate students but to reassure them that academic integrity is a vital priority of the course.

These strategies will encourage academic honesty by creating a situation in which cheating is very difficult and the fear of failure cannot prevail over the student's integrity. At the outset, some of these strategies may seem time-consuming or strict; however, they require only modest additional efforts by educators and students. These suggestions are based on experiences in a General Chemistry class, but can be applied to any large class setting in which academic integrity is essential. By taking these preemptive measures, educators can prevent students from undergoing the humiliating process of punishment for academic dishonesty; but more importantly, we can also encourage honest academic practices.

Notes

1. I would like to thank Dr. Gershon Vincow and Dr. Tess Freedman for helping me to evolve as an educator and providing the foundations on which most of these strategies were built. I would also like to thank Dr. Michael Sponsler for allowing me to pursue an opportunity that is not directly related to my research but will help further my academic career.

Appendix

The table below gives summarizes the Academic Integrity (AI) strategies proposed in this chapter.

Strategy	When to implement the strategy	Short description
Reserve extra testing space	Up to a year before the class—this most likely will involve the registrar	Reserve an extra room to allow students to sit at least a seat apart
Include AI section in the syllabus	At least one week before class starts	Include the academic integrity policy in the syllabus
Make an AI agreement sheet	At least one week before class starts	The sheet should include a line for the students' signatures
Discuss the policy	The first day of class	Emphasize the importance of the policy and collect signatures
Make attendance a reward	Sporadically throughout the semester, as an agreement reminder	Use a sign-in sheet to save time—use positive reinforcement
Determine the number of proctors needed	1-2 weeks before an exam—at most 25 students for each proctor	Be sure to alert each proctor of the date and time he or she is needed
Announce what will be tested	1-2 class periods before an exam	Be specific about what is allowed (calculator, reference sheets, etc.)
Announce if extra material will be provided	1-2 class periods before an exam (and again during the exam)	State what tables, charts, constants, etc., will be provided
Make different versions of exams	At least 1 week before an exam	This makes it hard for students to copy multiple-choice answers
Meet with proctors	30-40 minutes before an exam	To explain what is expected (active proctoring, how to check ID, etc.)
Check/clear calculators	Immediately before the exam	Do random calculator checks or clear all RAM
Seat students apart	At the beginning of an exam	Every other seat and row (this depends on room/class size)
Provide an academic testing environment	From the beginning of the exam and throughout the exam	Remove all papers, books, etc.; turn off all unnecessary electronics
Active proctoring	Throughout an exam	Proctors should move around, be alert, and answer questions

Strategy	When to implement the strategy	Short description
Communication between rooms	Throughout an exam	Have a messenger or phone access to communicate with other rooms
Announce reminders of "No Cheating"	During an exam	To further discourage cheating
ID students	After an exam	Ask to see ID as the students hand in the exams

Applying Intercultural Concepts to Academic Integrity

Michael Smithee

THE PREVIOUS CHAPTERS on academic integrity have provided you with explanations of theory, classroom policies, establishment and enforcement of policies, and practical issues. This chapter will explore some cultural and behavioral issues related to academic integrity. It will not, however, focus on specific countries or cultures at the risk of stereotyping or unfairly treating them. You will find that books on academic integrity scarcely mention the effect of culture on cheating and plagiarism. Journal articles giving more detailed explanations are available but rare. In the Works Cited and Resources sections of this chapter you will find some citations for further research.

"Welcome to My Culture" Is Not Enough

Cheating in U.S. institutions may have a different character than cheating in institutions outside of the U.S. One young teacher of English in a foreign country expressed his disgust by writing the following:

> In my two years of teaching, I routinely caught my students copying each others' homework, baldly plagiarizing off the Internet, surreptitiously hiding their books during an exam, attempting to bully a smarter student into sharing his work, or simply good old-fashioned leaning over his neighbor's desk to see what the answer was. (Schiavenza, 2007)

He went on to say,

> A friend of mine once taught a film studies course at a teacher's college

... and she often caught her students plagiarizing what should have been the easiest of assignments: writing a film review. She was flabbergasted that her students thought she couldn't tell the difference between a Roger Ebert essay and [those of] second-year ... college students.

Do cultural differences in academic habits mean the international student is more likely to cheat? Not necessarily. Even though most international students, like their American counterparts, understand that cheating is considered wrong by the authorities in academia, some of them may engage in it for such personal reasons as stress, fear of failure, expectations from parents, pressures from class bullies, and so on. One faculty member put her answer to this reality this way:

As an anthropologist I accept that other cultures conceptualize things like cheating differently. I have no problem accepting this, but I still say: so what? In my culture I explain what cheating is and when you do it in my class I flunk you and recommend to the dean of students that you be expelled. Welcome to my culture. (Throw, 2007)

She implies, "when in Rome, do as the Romans do." And I agree with this, *as long as the student knows what the "Romans" do and how and why they do it.* Because culture shock may play a part, this process of learning U.S. academic cultural nuances may take some international students longer than others. In terms of culture's effect on academic integrity, today's faculty find themselves in the position of teaching in intercultural classrooms.[1] For this reason, simply knowing one's discipline is insufficient. One needs intercultural awareness and competence (Chen & Starosta, 2003; Spitsberg, 2004; Sapp, 2002; Powell & Andersen, 1994; Lieberman, 1994).

Today's faculty find themselves in the position of teaching in intercultural classrooms. For this reason, simply knowing one's discipline is insufficient. One needs intercultural awareness and competence.

To understand fully any individual student's response to cheating and plagiarism, faculty, departments, staff, and students sitting in judgment need to understand their own levels of intercultural competence. Chen and Starosta (2003, 344) explain the importance of three interrelated components: (1) intercultural sensitivity, the *affective* approach that focuses on the readiness to understand and appreciate cultural differences, (2) intercultural awareness, the *cognitive* approach that focuses on the understanding of cultural conventions that affect thinking and behavior, and (3) intercultural adroitness, the *behavioral* approach that focuses on the skills involved in intercultural interactions. An apparent lack of such understanding is why Throw's "welcome to my culture" is an insufficient response in the global classroom.

Proposed Axioms

These and other critiques and comments have led me to propose some axioms about academic integrity. These may not be comprehensive, but they provide some notion of the common characteristics of academic integrity in the U.S. and around the world, and are worth discussing with students, professors, and colleagues.

- No culture condones cheating.
- Some cultures are more lax than others in their interpretations and enforcement of rules on cheating.
- Some students from cultures in which there is corruption at the institutional and faculty levels may be bolder in their cheating practices.
- The mindset of international students coming to the U.S. includes notions about the practices of learning and concepts used in those learning processes, many of which may differ from those common in the U.S. classroom.
- Rules about cheating in the U.S. classroom are formulated to mesh with specific cultural practices involving a specific mindset.
- The boundaries for establishing what counts as cheating are constantly stretched, both by those who understand the language and by those who don't.
- Descriptions and explanations of what constitutes cheating will be misinterpreted, misapplied, and misplaced (unconsciously or consciously) by American students as well as by international students, but potentially for different reasons.
- Attitudes about cheating vary greatly both within the American culture and among cultures globally.

The axioms proposed above do not absolve anyone for having cheated. With some exceptions, all academic institutions treat cheating as a serious matter. However, I propose that faculty and peers of accused students withhold judgment until a full and impartial review of an alleged incident has been made. Institutional procedures exist to determine whether an alleged infraction is *intentional* or *unintentional* (Lathrop & Foss, 2000, 162-3), *cultural* or *personal*

(Storti, 1999, 15-7). This is often a judgment call based on input from a variety of people and a review of the circumstances.

"Contrast-American" Assumptions and Values

In each culture, there are normative cultural assumptions, values, attitudes, and behaviors. *International students* who enroll in any course of study must understand these normative constructs and how they may contrast with the norms of their home countries. It is also vital that *faculty* understand normative ideas about themselves and about the students from other cultures with whom they interact. Of course, there is a difficulty. No one can know all of the assumptions and values of another culture, let alone all other cultures. International student advisors and faculty who interact frequently with international students come closer than most in this respect. As regards academic integrity, much difficulty can be avoided by attending to the front end of the issue: understanding the concepts that drive faculty members' and students' own behavior.

Stewart, Danielian, and Foster (1998) offer an extensive and diverse set of cultural *assumptions* and *values*. A few samples from this set that may affect academic integrity appear below. The authors summarize their findings in a table juxtaposing American and "contrast-American" assumptions and values, grouped into six conceptual categories:

- definition of activity,
- definition of social relations,
- motivation,
- perception of the world,
- perception of the self and the individual, and
- generalized forms. (167-71)

For example, in the "definition of activity" category, one finds the common American value of active (student-centered) learning paired with the contrast-American concept of passive (rote) learning. I have chosen a few concepts to illustrate the linking of cultural variance to academic integrity. The "contrast-American" assumptions and values that affect academic integrity include (but are not limited to) the following.

Definition of Social Relations

Relationships. "Contrast-American" interpersonal relationships are person centered rather than task centered. They tend to be few but enduring. Some, such as friendships, can be established from childhood. Relationships are often considered long term rather than based on a temporary situation such as rooming together in a dormitory.

Social obligations. Such obligations are inherent in friendship, but also extend to other social situations. These are not usually flexible, and are rarely expressed in written, legal terms. Thus, there is pressure to help others even if it means cheating.

Collective responsibility. The group one identifies with may also share the shame if one does not succeed.

Perception of the World

Connection. In many cultures one perceives oneself as part of nature rather than detached, as part of a hierarchy rather than apart from any hierarchy. This perception forces the individual to perceive the self as subject to forces above himself or herself in the hierarchy. Such a perception leads to a tendency to obey others who are perceived to be higher ranking. Those who perceive themselves as detached from nature may not automatically accept as truth something stated by someone of higher rank.

Perception of the Self and the Individual

Self-reliance. In contrast to American norms, many other cultures encourage reliance on a variety of groups, such as superiors, patrons, parents, and friends. The individual should not stand alone but should seek help when in need. When help is received from people other than friends and other close relations, there may be obligations to be repaid. Thus, sharing homework or getting extra help from faculty may incur an obligation.

This is but a brief sampling of the many assumptions and values identified by Stewart, Danielian, and Foster. The reader is encouraged to review this resource for a more detailed discussion of these aspects of culture to gain an understanding of how one's own assumptions and values may differ from others', and may guide the reasoning underlying one's behaviors.

Language and Ambiguity

LaRay Barna (1994) discusses *language differences* as potential barriers to communication. These are also relevant to academic integrity. The miscommunications that can occur among students for whom English is a second language are well known. It takes years for some students to master the level of English needed to produce a dissertation. In addition, the way in which directions are expressed by faculty may confuse some students for whom English is a second language because of a tendency to interpret what is being said in terms of their own cultural concepts. Some educators reject the notion that lack of familiarity with English excuses the misunderstanding of classroom instructions. They maintain that foreigners must know the language before coming to the U.S. However, in my thirty years of experience with international students, I have found that it takes one to two semesters for them to be able to speak and grasp the local version of English. This is often the case even for students having a TOEFL score of 600 or better.

Similarly, ambiguity can be a factor in misunderstanding. A directive from a professor may appear to the non-native English speaker as unclear due to the way the word translates into his or her native language, or to the various meanings the word may have when translated, or to the context in which the directive was given. In this way, students from high-context cultures, in which meaning comes from *how* something is said as much or more than from the actual words used,[2] may interpret directives according to their own cultural nuances.

For example, a professor may say "you will neither give nor receive help on this take-home test." The concept of "receiving help" might not be the same for some international students as for American students. The international student could infer that contact with other students should cease once he or she sits down to write the answers, or that help is only inappropriate when given in the context of answering questions, not in the process of understanding the topic. An international student from a society in which friendship and group norms are stronger than the individualistic norms of American society might

> *Faculty members need to be aware of the cultural aspects of friendship and communication, and discuss with students their understanding of cultural norms relative to the instructions given for an exam.*

wonder, "Does this mean I cannot ask my friend the meaning of some words in the test question? Does this mean that I can discuss this *topic* with my friend, but *not the test question*? Or does it mean that I can ask my friend how the question may be interpreted, but not the answer to the question?"

To our hypothetical student, having the friend say in regard to the test question, "this goes here, and that goes there" might be considered "helping," which of course would be cheating. But, in the same case, the international student might think that it would be acceptable to review his understanding of the topic, or even the meaning of the question, with a friend, and that this would not be considered giving or receiving help. Such a student lacks the cultural experience to assume, on the basis of the test-taking situation, the need to cease asking all questions about the topic. It is incumbent on the professor to provide clarification, *in advance*. Faculty members need to be aware of the cultural aspects of communication, and discuss with students their understanding of cultural norms relative to the instructions given for an exam.

However, problems may arise from the ongoing nature of study and communication between friends. Students who have consistently studied together are likely to have a similar understanding of the topic, which can lead to nearly identical written responses on an exam. In such a case, the faculty member must assess whether the students cheated after the rules were laid down, or whether previous study produced the resemblance. This could involve an oral follow-up to the exam.

Asking Questions

A common cultural problem for many international students has to do with asking questions, a critical behavior in American classrooms. In some countries, asking questions is either forbidden or discouraged, as questioning the professor may be perceived as a challenge to authority. Among peers, asking questions can also be considered stupid: stupid for making the professor lose face, or stupid in revealing a failure to understand the material as initially delivered. In rare cases where the professor really does want to have questions asked, peers might consider it "brown nosing" or seeking to win points with the professor at the expense of other students.

To overcome these inhibitions, professors should make students aware that questions can be asked through a variety of media: aloud in class, privately during office hours, and by email. Students should be encouraged to ask questions in a variety of ways and for a variety of reasons:

- If the information makes you wonder about its meaning, then you need to ask a question.
- If after the professor has said something, you wonder "why," then you need to ask a question.
- If you have never heard a term or phrase the professor uses, then you need to ask a question.
- If you are in the habit of collaborating closely with friends on your work, then you need to ask a question about when working with friends is acceptable, as violating these rules can lead to shame for both you and your friends.

Conclusion and Suggestions

Do not accept culture alone as an excuse for cheating, but do explore and keep an open mind about cultural differences, language issues, and behavioral norms that may be contributing factors. What is clear for a professor is not always clear to a student, even if the student is encouraged to ask questions.

There are many steps that faculty can take to reduce the risk that issues of academic integrity involving international students will arise:

- Recognize that culture plays a role in international and domestic student behavior.
- Consult with foreign students' advisors, faculty from other countries, and experienced international students about perceptions related to cheating and plagiarism.
- Support efforts on campus to prevent cheating.
- Explore their own cultural assumptions and values for biases that inform their behavior.
- Acknowledge before each exam, project, or paper that there is often pressure to cheat, and discuss ways to overcome this.
- Discuss their methods of grading.
- Acknowledge the seriousness of cheating by reviewing the axioms proposed above with students.
- Explain their definitions, policies, and processes related to cheating and plagiarism.
- Avoid the trap of assuming "we're all adults and we know that cheating is forbidden"—this does not go far enough toward understanding the motivations and circumstances that lead to "cheating" behaviors.

The list of American/contrast-American assumptions and values found in Stewart, Danielian, and Foster and the discussion of barriers to communication found in Barna highlight the strength of differences between cultures, the possibilities for complex mixings of these values, and the number of potential reasons for people to engage in cheating and plagiarism. When a student is found cheating, faculty and honor courts generally invoke expectations based on assumptions and values characteristic of an American university. However, American institutions do not, ostensibly, accept people from abroad for the purpose of changing their identity or cultural character (although this may happen as a by-product). Indeed, most American universities recognize the vital contribution of international students to their mission as centers of learning in a pluralistic and globalized world. It is thus the responsibility of the American university to minimize cultural barriers relating to academic integrity. This enhances the possibilities of success for institutions, academic departments, professors, and students.

Notes

1. The term faculty will be used to refer to all who provide classroom or web-based instruction, unless the context dictates otherwise.

2. A discussion of the concept of high-context cultures can be found in Hall (1976). High-context cultures are contrasted with low-context cultures, in which the communication is in the words and little else. Hall uses Japan as an example of a high-context culture and the United States as an example of a low-context culture.

Works Cited

Barna, L. M. (1994). Stumbling blocks in intercultural communication. In L. A. Samovar & R. E. Porter (Eds.), *Intercultural communication: A reader* (7th ed., pp. 337-346). Belmont, CA: Wadsworth.

Chen, G., & Starosta, W. (2003). Intercultural awareness. In L. A. Samovar & R. E. Porter (Eds.), *Intercultural communication: A reader* (7th ed., pp. 344-353). Belmont, CA: Wadsworth.

Hall, E. T. (1976). *Beyond culture.* Garden City, NY: Anchor.

Lathrop, A., & Foss., K. (2000). *Student cheating and plagiarism in the Internet era: A wake-up call.* Englewood, CO: Libraries Unlimited.

Lieberman, D. A. (1994). Ethnocognitivism, problem solving, and hemisphericity. In L. A. Samovar & R. E. Porter (Eds.), *Intercultural communication: A reader* (7th ed., pp. 178-193). Belmont, CA: Wadsworth.

Powell, R. G., & Andersen, J. F. (1994). Culture and classroom communication. In L. A. Samovar & R. E. Porter (Eds.), *Intercultural communication: A reader* (7th ed., pp. 322-330). Belmont, CA: Wadsworth.

Schiavenza, M. (2007, November 5). A *China journal.* Available at http://www.mattschiavenza.com/?p=98

Sapp, D. A. (2002). Towards an international and intercultural understanding of plagiarism and academic dishonesty in composition: Reflections from the People's Republic of China. *Issues in Writing, 13*(1), 58-79.

Spitzberg, B. H. (2004). A model of intercultural communication competence. In L. A. Samovar & R. E. Porter (Eds.), *Intercultural communication: A reader* (7th ed., pp. 347-359). Belmont, CA: Wadsworth.

Stewart, E. C., Danielian, J., & Foster, R. J. (1998). Cultural assumptions and values. In M. J. Bennett (Ed.), *Basic concepts of intercultural communication:*

Selected readings (pp. 157-172). Yarmouth, ME: Intercultural Press.

Storti, C. (1999). *Figuring foreigners out: A practical guide.* Yarmouth, ME: Intercultural Press.

Throw, A. (2007, May 24). Welcome to my culture [posted comment]. In Elizabeth Redden, *Cheating across cultures.* Available at http://www.insidehighered.com/news/2007/05/24/cheating

Resources

Althen, G. (1995). *The handbook of international student advising* (Rev. ed.). Yarmouth, ME: Intercultural Press.

Bennett, M. J. (Ed.). (1998). *Basic concepts of intercultural communication: Selected readings.* Yarmouth, ME: Intercultural Press.

Cizek, G. J. (2003). *Detecting and preventing classroom cheating: Promoting integrity in assessment,* Thousand Oaks, CA: Corwin.

Crabtree, R. D., & Sapp, D. A. (2004). Your culture, my classroom, whose pedagogy? Negotiating effective teaching and learning in Brazil. *Journal of Studies in International Education, 8*(1), 105-132.

Decoo, W. (2002). *Crisis on campus: Confronting academic misconduct.* Cambridge, MA: MIT Press.

Hall, E. T. (1976). *Beyond culture.* Garden City, NY: Anchor.

Hayes, N., & Introna, L. (2005). Cultural values, plagiarism, and fairness: When plagiarism gets in the way of learning. *Ethics & Behavior, 15*(3), 213-231.

Hofstede, G. (1997). *Cultures and organizations: Software of the mind* (Rev. ed.). New York: McGraw Hill.

Samovar, L. A., & Porter, R. E. (Eds.). (1994). *Intercultural communication: A reader* (7th ed.). Belmont, CA: Wadsworth.

Smithee, M., Greenblatt, S. L., & Eland, A. (2004). *U.S. classroom culture.* Washington, DC: NAFSA, Association of International Educators.

Stewart, E. C., & Bennett, M. J. (1991). *American cultural patterns: A cross-cultural perspective* (Rev. ed.). Yarmouth, ME: Intercultural Press.

Storti, C. (1990). *The art of crossing cultures,* Yarmouth, ME: Intercultural Press.

Whitley, B. E., Jr., & Keith-Spiegel, P. (2002). *Academic dishonesty: An educator's guide.* Mahwah, NJ: Lawrence Erlbaum Associates.

The Dreaded Laboratory Report

Danielle Schuehler Sherwood

THE NEMESIS OF MY undergraduate studies was the dreaded lab report. There were several reasons I found the lab report so daunting:

1. I had to understand several pages of technical background information and then reword it into an *introduction* section of the lab report material.
2. Calculations had to be done with the *data*, then analyzed and *discussed*.
3. There were *questions* to answer.
4. A *conclusion* had to be written.

Although I did not realize this when I was an undergraduate, as a teaching assistant (TA), I have found that the reason the lab report was so challenging has to do with academic integrity. In my capacity as a TA evaluating lab reports, I have found that integrity concerns arise related to each of the points that I outlined above. More specifically, taking the text and data sections into consideration separately allows for a discussion on how to give direction to the students to improve the quality of both their learning and their work.

The Written Material: Introduction, Questions, Discussion, and Conclusion

Similar issues arise with the different "text sections" of the lab report, which include the introduction, questions, discussion, and conclusion. In these sections, the students must write about technical information. Within the text sections of a lab report, there are two common problems: 1) direct plagiarism from the lab manual or textbook, particularly for the introduction, and 2) identical written material from multiple students.

The major reason why students copy from the lab manual, particularly for the introduction to a lab report, is feeling overwhelmed by the report. The second most common section that is plagiarized is the answers to the questions. Just as I found the lab report daunting as an undergraduate, my students have told me that they feel the same way. Directly using sections of the text from the manual without summarizing or rewording is a faster way to write the introduction and answer questions, because they do not need to first comprehend the information.

> *The major reason why students copy is feeling overwhelmed. Directly using sections of the text from the manual without summarizing or rewording is faster, because they do not need to first comprehend the information.*

Of particular note in the TA's responsibilities is the task of informing students about the acceptable use of the lab manual, because one might think this chore should be done by the professor. The professor of the course will usually have the policy outlined in his or her syllabus; however, the TA is the person who deals with the practical application of this guiding principle. Ensuring that the TA has made the policy clear means that the student cannot say, "Oh, you never told me that." It is a way of eliminating one of the many excuses that students like to use when they have been caught cheating.

A useful strategy to discourage students from copying from the textbook is to make use of the pre-lab lecture. In most labs, the TA talks at the beginning for 10 to 15 minutes to help familiarize the students with the theoretical concepts involved in the lab and any procedural details. During this time, it is essential to make the theory as simple as possible so that students really understand the essence of the lab and can describe back to you what they are doing in the procedure. I have found that giving them a handout with the pre-lab lecture notes on it helps them to listen to the lecture rather than concentrate on writing down every word I say. When asked if these handouts were helpful, one student said, "Yes, I really like that you write out all the important information for the pre-lab so that when you talk about it, I can focus on the actual idea rather than trying to write everything down. Really helpful!" After all, this is the reason that students take lab: to obtain a practical and hands-on understanding of a theoretical concept that was taught during lecture, not to take notes.

The discussion part of the lab is unique and encourages student collaboration, leading to the second kind of textual plagiarism: copying each others' work. From my experience, the discussion is the hardest part of the lab report, because you need to understand the theoretical information and procedure in order to process your results. In this section, students are forced to make their own analytical statements about the results. They need to answer the critical question of how theoretical values relate to results and to use their own judgment about how experimental factors have influenced these results. Thus, no two students, even lab partners who have worked together, should have the same discussion. Identical discussions indicate that students have not done their work independently and are in violation of academic integrity policies.

While it might be tempting to conclude that identical lab reports are the result of laziness or not understanding the lab, hard-working students may produce identical reports for multiple reasons. During the experimental part of the lab, students are allowed to work with partners; it is likely that some students, perhaps not realizing it is not allowed, continue to work with their lab partners outside of class on the lab report, which can result in identical reports. This is often the case with the discussion, conclusion, and questions, because these cannot be copied from the manual. The case of students having the same lab report is difficult to deal with because TAs do not know if both people were equal contributors or if one person did the work and the other copied. Therefore, it is crucial to make it clear to students in the syllabus and by verbal communication that each student must turn in his or her own unique lab report. *It is your responsibility as a TA to make sure that students know what is and what is not acceptable to use from the manual and from other students.*

Most professors will have a standard policy for dealing with these infringements of academic integrity. The TA's responsibility is to recognize these violations. Before grading labs, the TA should be very familiar with the lab manual text to be able to recognize if an introduction has been copied. Additionally, the TA should try to grade the lab reports within a short time period so that he or she is familiar with the students' reports and can recognize if two are the same. When a TA is grading a lab report and finds sections directly copied from the text, he or she must first talk to the student before passing the issue along to the professor of the class.

The data section of the lab report is completely different, because this section requires students to analyze their results. The critical point in the data section is to ensure that the students are accurately reporting their results, which can be achieved by the point distribution of the lab, by signing data before students leave the lab, or even by requiring the submission of the results before they leave the room.

The Non-Textual Part: The Data

Unlike the text of the lab report, the data cannot be directly copied from the lab manual, and several students can have identical numbers, since they worked together to generate the results. The issue at hand is accuracy in reporting those results. It is not uncommon to find that a student has changed his or her results to make it look as if almost 100% of the desired product was obtained or that the values measured perfectly match those expected theoretically. This problem is of particular importance since some of the students in lab are the researchers of tomorrow.

One strategy I use to discourage students from changing their results is to give more points for the analysis of the results than the actual numbers, which stresses to students that explaining the results is much more important than obtaining perfect results in the first place. In reality, the only way a student can lose credit on the data section of his or her lab is by not writing down a number. This way, there is no incentive to change the results. Additionally, the point of lab is to learn a technique, which means a student probably will not be very good at it the first time he or she tries.

The focus on explanation in lab reports is a way to encourage academic integrity when the students transfer their class skills to real research. In my work with undergraduate students doing original research, they often find their first several weeks to be very discouraging, because the desired results are not obtained on the first or second try as happens in the undergraduate teaching laboratory. It becomes very tempting for them to lie about their research results. Therefore, helping students to learn that experiments do not always "work" in class promotes academic integrity in both the short and the long term.

Encouraging good analysis rather than penalizing poor results is helpful to prevent students from increasing their yields or otherwise improving their results. A TA can also support honest reporting by monitoring the data during the lab. For example, I noticed that some students leave the laboratory with no results recorded, which allows them to improve the results without needing to change the data sheet. Once, when I asked a person in one group where his results were, he told me he was going to get together with his lab partners later. This is certainly not the point of lab, to have students teaming up with partners later to make up perfect data.

Encouraging good analysis rather than penalizing poor results is helpful to prevent students from increasing their yields or otherwise improving their results.

Another time, when grading a lab, I discovered that a lab group of two students doing the same experiment reported radically different yields—one 98% and the other 62%. The first lab partner had forgotten to let his partner know he had improved the results he was reporting! Thus, at minimum, a TA needs to look at students' results before they leave class. An even better strategy is to require students to hand in a copy of their results before leaving or to put a stamp or signature (in a uniquely colored pen) directly on students' data to ensure that they have each recorded the results and cannot change them at a later date.

It is possible that a student could purposely write down a number while in lab that is better than the one he or she actually obtained. This can be discouraged by the TA having an active presence in the lab, such as walking around the room and communicating with students about their results while they are doing the lab. This attention to the students' activity will make them less likely (and less able) to cheat. Additionally, these short conversations with students give them an opportunity to ask questions about the material, thereby helping to prevent other integrity concerns like a plagiarized introduction or a copied discussion.

As with the written sections of the lab report, the TA must make clear to the students at the beginning of the semester that accurate reporting of the data is critical. Even more so than with regard to written sections, a TA must talk with a student found to have falsified his or her results. Unchecked, falsified results in many research fields have devastating results.

The Penalties for Infringements of Academic Integrity

The strategies outlined in this chapter have the intent of reducing issues of academic integrity, but if a TA does have a problem, most professors will have a standard policy for dealing with these infringements of academic integrity. The TA's responsibility is to recognize these violations. Talking with the professor in charge of the lab will clarify his or her policy.

Getting the Right Results: The Role of the TA

In the scientific community, accurately communicating results is as important as obtaining them. Although daunting for students to write and for TAs to grade, the laboratory report is an import component of undergraduate study. Since this report serves as training for a career in the fields of science, it is critical to demand academic integrity with this report. The following is a timeline for implementing the strategies:

- On the first day of class, give clear instructions to students about what is and is not acceptable to copy from the text and from other students.
- Before they begin testing, give students a clear understanding of the theoretical background of the experiment to dissuade them from copying the text, which includes handing out pre-lab notes in hard copy to the students.

- Have an active presence in the lab.
- Keep a copy of the results or sign data sheets to encourage integrity.
- Grade lab reports within a short amount of time to recognize reports that are the same.
- Emphasize accurate reporting of results by giving more points for good analysis than for the results themselves.

Although the lab report will certainly continue to be the nemesis of students who think going out with friends is more important than writing the report, encouraging academic integrity will make the exercise good training for the real world, where there is little a scientist does that is more important than communicating through written results. As a professor recently told me, "Our job is to inform students about the issues of academic integrity and to make an environment that discourages plagiarism so they choose not to cheat. Preventing cheating is better than catching them after the fact." Doing so will make science students into scientists.

Detecting and Preventing Cheating During Exams

Kevin Yee and Patricia MacKown

THE CENTER FOR Academic Integrity at Clemson University (previously at Duke University) reports that "on most campuses, over 75% of students admit to some cheating. In a 1999 survey of 2,100 students on 21 campuses across the country, about *one third* of the participating students admitted to serious test cheating." Given this, it seems wise that we, as educators, learn as much as possible about cheating methods used by students.

While the University of Central Florida (UCF), like any large university, uncovers its share of cheating by students, formal statistics on cheating methods are not presently kept. However, informally brainstorming about instructors' past experiences with student cheating methods has often proved useful in the training of new teaching assistants and adjunct faculty members, and the list of possible cheating styles presented in this chapter grew organically from such humble beginnings. While UCF did not gather statistics on the frequency of teachers observing or suspecting the employ of each method, the list grew with each new method observed or idea supplied by participants during brainstorming. In the past, we also did not inquire into how the future TAs and adjunct faculty members knew of these methods new to our list, but contented ourselves with having identified yet another technique. We are investigating possibly collecting data on both issues in the future, but here is what we have learned so far.

The dual notions of detection and prevention inform the current incarnation of the list. Our hope is not to merely identify, after the fact, how students are cheating, but to list possible measures that might aid in detecting students' academic dishonesty while it is in progress. After all, we are best able to catch cheaters if we know *how* they are cheating. Naturally, it is best of all to prevent cheating in the first place. Each method of cheating on the list lends itself to particular strategies in the classroom that, if enacted, would discourage students from even attempting to cheat. Indeed, a good testing environment benefits all students. A well-proctored, disciplined environment ensures fairness to everyone and provides comfort by assuring students that their academic achievements are being fairly measured. Cheating interferes with some of the best qualities of undergraduate education, including the intrinsic pursuit of knowledge and wisdom that an academic course of study normally encourages. Seen in this light, it behooves us as educators to do all we can to prevent it (minimize its presence), or failing that, to detect it (minimize its effectiveness). The very quality of undergraduate education depends on our success in this endeavor.

Using Other People

Cheating Method	Detection Method	Prevention
1. **Whispering:** asking for and giving answers verbally	Listen at all times for student whispering.	Use multiple proctors; wander continually; stand close to anyone whispering
2. **Wandering eyes:** looking over the shoulder of someone or to the side	Watch for wandering eyes, looking out of corner of eyes	Use multiple proctors; wander continually
3. **Passing notes:** scribbles on paper	Watch for contact between people	Leave empty chairs in between students
4. **Sign language:** use hand gestures (especially fingers for numbers) to communicate with others	Watch for movement of hands	Use multiple proctors; wander continually
5. **Morse code – voice:** use coughing or sneezing a set number of times to communicate an answer	Listen for rhythmic and repetitious noises; be wary of coughing	Demonstrate extra interest (go closer) when students cough
6. **Morse code – nonverbal:** use sounds like stamping feet, tapping pencil, etc. ,to communicate an answer	Listen for rhythmic and repetitious noises	Demonstrate extra interest (go closer) when rhythmic noises persist
7. **Misdirection:** one person distracts the proctor(s) while others cheat	Use multiple proctors; heightened alertness when a distraction occurs	Use multiple proctors; heightened alertness when a distraction occurs

Using the Body or Environment

Cheating Method	Detection Method	Prevention
8. **Write on body**: ink written on body part, perhaps covered by long sleeves	Watch for furtive movements. Beware not just sleeves, but under socks or even down shirts	Use multiple proctors; wander continually
9. **Write on desk**: especially when written in pencil for easy wiping later	Watch student eyes and hands; are they moving the test back and forth across the desk?	Examine desks before class, watch for scribbling just before test distribution
10. **Cheat sheet**: prewritten cheat sheet, usually small font, hidden in clothes or under wristwatch	Observe student hand movements	Use multiple proctors; wander continually; OR allow cheat sheets and design test for application, not facts
11. **Cheat sheet on floor**: prewritten cheat sheet hidden in book or under folders below the desk	Observe student foot movements; watch for students looking down	Require that books or notes be stored in backpack, not under desk
12. **Cheat sheet in bag**: prewritten cheat sheet in backpack; accessed when getting new pen	Beware of "fetching a new writing utensil or eraser"	Consider requiring bags be placed in a pile at the front of the room
13. **Bathroom**: leave with permission; get notes prehidden in bathroom (or from a friend waiting outside lecture hall)	Send a proctor to follow the student, within reason	Scan bathroom for hiding spots before test; OR do not allow bathroom breaks
14. **Chewing gum**: write cheats on stick of gum in ink; pop into mouth if endangered (evidence is gone)	Wander room continually	Use multiple proctors; wander continually—cheaters will get scared and eat gum sooner than if you never wandered
15. **Baby wipes**: write on the body in ink, but have an alcohol wipe ready to remove evidence quickly	Watch for students looking at skin under clothing or having moist towelettes handy	Wander hall BEFORE exam so cheaters get nervous and wipe away the cheats
16. **Invisible ink**: visible only with a certain kind of handheld pen light	Watch for a tiny light being used secretly	Patrol the room regularly
17. **Water bottle**: remove label, write cheats on inside with small font, reattach. Water acts as magnifying lens	Watch for students staring intently into water bottles	Require bottles remain on floor and not be used during the test

Using the Body or Environment (continued)

Cheating Method	Detection Method	Prevention
18. **Baseball cap:** reading the underside of the brim	Watch for wandering eyes	Remove all hats
19. **Sunglasses:** cheats pasted or written on inside of dark sunglasses	Observe carefully any sunglasses that stay on during the test	Remove all sunglasses
20. **Barrel pens:** pens with a small window and click to rotate messages can have a "safe" setting and use the other click settings to write cheats	Be suspicious of the pen-click noise	Stand near any student clicking abnormally
21. **Bra:** cheat sheet stuck into center of bra, visible only when looking down into blouse	Watch student eye movements	Use multiple proctors; wander continually
22. **Leg fan:** cheat sheet folded like a fan and taped inside thighs; student hikes up skirt and opens legs, and cheats are visible only to the cheater	Watch student eye movements	Use multiple proctors; wander continually

Using Technology

Cheating Method	Detection Method	Prevention
23. **Cell – texting:** type out a text message to someone else in class (or even at home) and get silent text reply	Watch for cell phone usage of any kind	Prohibit cell phones in test environment
24. **Cell – photo:** take photo of test question, send to someone at home, get silent text reply	Watch for cell phone usage of any kind	Prohibit cell phones in test environment
25. **Calculator – program:** type formulas or cheats into calculator before test begins	Patrol room frequently; watch for frantic clearing of calculator results; watch for "flipping through" calculator read-out	Prohibit calculators in test environment; OR ask department to invest in a box of "simple" calculators to share for tests
26. **Calculator – sharing:** program cheats ahead of time and let someone else use the calculator during the test	Watch for sharing of calculators	Prohibit calculators in test environment; OR ask department to invest in a box of "simple" calculators to share for tests
27. **iPod – professor:** listen to recorded lecture during the test; possible to hide earphone wires behind long hair	Scan for earphone wires; patrol room nonstop	Prohibit iPod usage; require devices to be placed into backpack below desk
28. **iPod – student:** pre-record yourself saying formulas and cheats; listen during test	Scan for earphone wires; patrol room nonstop	Prohibit iPod usage; require devices to be placed into backpack below desk

Other Methods

Cheating Method	Detection Method	Prevention
29. **Mutilate:** erase, cross out, crease, fold, cover over (even with Chapstick) "non-answer" parts of the Scantron form to confuse the machine and guarantee a 100% score (note: none of these methods work all the time)	Watch for any alterations of Scantron form	Patrol the room often; erase any pencil markings over the pre-printed black lines along the side of the Scantron (the most common method); hand-score any suspicious Scantrons.
30. **Shades of gray:** guess about multiple answers in the same line, all in gray so you have a chance to get lucky. Also possible to erase the wrong answers if you get the form back, and make a case for the machine not seeing your answer	Give a cursory glance to all Scantrons before being scored; make a note of students who left multiple answers potentially filled in; it helps to photocopy such Scantrons before scoring them, as a record	Do not hand back Scantrons; report student grades to them electronically instead
31. **Lie about answer:** Leave answer blank entirely, but bubble in the correct answer in "gray" when the form comes back, and claim the machine didn't read it	Make a photocopy of any Scantrons that have blank spaces	Do not hand back Scantrons; report student grades to them electronically instead
32. **Duplicate Scantrons:** have a friend take the test on two forms but keep one. In next hour, you turn in his/her form as your own	Watch for someone filling in two Scantrons during the test, perhaps one on top of the other.	Use a different version of the test for each class section (or at least reorder the questions)
33. **Steal questions:** keep the question packet and give it to someone who will take the test later in the day	Watch how students pack up at the end of the test, and keep an eye out for questions being stuffed into bags	Require return of questions; verify that every student turning in answers also turns in question sheet
34. **Bank Questions:** memorize questions from last year's test, saved by a friend or a social (Greek) organization	Detect pattern of sudden perfect scores for a student whose grades were much worse previously	Change the test every semester—more than just the order of questions!

Other Methods (continued)

Cheating Method	Detection Method	Prevention
35. **Publisher's questions:** contact the textbook publisher and pose as an instructor; request test bank	Detect pattern of sudden perfect scores for a student whose grades were much worse previously	Don't use the publisher's test bank
36. **Feign Illness:** after seeing test, get permission to go home sick and take the same test later	Detect pattern of sudden perfect scores for a student whose grades were much worse previously	Use different questions on make-up exams
37. **Ringer:** send in an expert to take the test for you and write down your name	Check ID when Scantron is handed in	Tell students you will check ID when Scantron is handed in

Reading this list, one is struck by patterns that repeat multiple times. Detecting student cheating is often a matter of being extremely aware of where the students are looking, which implies a need to watch their eyes almost constantly (this may also prove to be the most effective method of prevention, as they will be aware of the extra attention). For this reason, among others, proctors are strongly advised to avoid bringing along any work of their own to the exam.

The other pattern that leaps out from the list is one of noise and distraction. Proctors need to use their ears as well as their eyes. While whispering may be one of the most common forms of cheating, it is hardly the most complicated method. iPods raise the ante, but more prosaic methods involve misdirection and multiple students forming a distraction. Any sound disruptions in the room should heighten the proctor's alertness.

When it comes to preventing cheating, which ought to be the real goal, much of this advice calls for proctors to roam the test room frequently. For large classes, the use of multiple proctors is highly encouraged. Instructors in the same discipline or department might agree to help each other proctor for free as a joint service. Proctoring actively is a full-time activity that requires complete concentration to be done effectively. As a proctor, one should give full attention to the classroom anyway, to be available to answer student questions and to reinforce the impression that students and their work environment are the top priority.

Works Cited

Center for Academic Integrity, Rutland Institute for Ethics, Clemson University. Available at http://www.academicintegrity.org

What's the Deal with Turnitin?

Tyra Twomey

What It Is and Why You Should Care: A Quick Overview

Turnitin is the best known, and one of the longest running, of today's commercially available plagiarism detection services (although the company advertises itself these days as a "Digital Assessment Suite"). Essentially, educators (and students) at subscribing institutions can submit written work to the site to have it "tested" for duplicated strings of words—"matches" between submitted text and both text accessible on the web and the text of all previously submitted papers, which are archived in an immense database. Submitted papers are returned to educators (or students) with "matched" text highlighted and information provided about the matching material. The company's sales brochure offers the following brief introduction to its services:

> Turnitin allows educators to check students' work for improper citation or potential plagiarism by comparing it against continuously updated databases using the industry's most advanced search technology. Every Originality Report provides instructors with the opportunity to teach their students proper citation methods as well as to safeguard their students' academic integrity. (Turnitin.com, n.d.)

Syracuse University is one of many universities, colleges, and high schools internationally who subscribe to the service. Depending on their departments, curricula, and the individual decisions made by their cooperating instructors, TAs may opt to use the service—or may be required to. Because its adoption and use remain somewhat controversial, it is a good idea for teachers and TAs to have some familiarity with Turnitin whether or not they will be using it.[1]

The Plagiarism Detection Controversy: Pros, Cons, and Lawyers

At first glance, plagiarism detection services might seem like a godsend to frustrated professors and busy TAs. Even when their more problematic attributes are brought to light, the value they can offer as a timesaving device and source-use checker remains significant. Anyone who has ever tried to Google-search suspicious word string after suspicious word string to find the one instance in which a dishonest writer was careless enough not to replace enough words with synonyms knows what a time-consuming process "plagiarism detection" can be when practiced on a case-by-case basis, and instructors of large sections often simply lack the time to follow up on every questionable sentence that crosses their desks.

The use of a plagiarism detection service can thus serve two highly beneficial purposes for such instructors: in the short term, it can enable them to check out every concern they have, not just the few they have time for, so that they can more accurately distinguish between students who *have* done the work correctly and those who have not. In the long term, such an option makes it feasible for them to continue to assign and grade pedagogically valuable research papers and other written work, instead of relying on such dubious assessment tools as easily scanned multiple choice tests, to gauge student progress.

Additionally, most plagiarism detection services can be used to check for language-matching in working drafts, not only final papers, and so can be put to use to help teach citation and paraphrasing practices (see the next section for more on how). Unfortunately, however, these benefits alone do not tell the whole story.

Most plagiarism detection services can be used to check for language-matching in working drafts, not only final papers, and so can be put to use to help teach citation and paraphrasing practices.

The most frequently cited objection to a school's adoption and use of such a service is that it conveys to student writers an institutional expectation of their criminality. By telling students we will be checking all papers for plagiarism, we are essentially calling them all cheaters before they have even begun to write, and treating them as if they are "guilty until proven innocent" by the returned results of electronic surveillance. Although proponents of the service argue that honest students have nothing to fear from such surveillance, others worry about the damage such an emphasis on policing can do to the climate of trust and exchange they feel should characterize an institution of learning.

Another key objection is the concern that allowing teachers to develop a reliance on such quick-fix services will act as a disincentive for teachers to develop and implement sounder, more time-consuming pedagogical practices. A far better way to prevent plagiarism, some argue, is by *teaching ethical writing:* instructing students in disciplinary conventions and expectations, textual ethics, cultural ideas about authorship, responsible critical research, and the rationales and practices of correct citation and source attribution. Additionally, opponents of the service point out that unique, creatively designed writing assignments tend to generate unique, creative responses, while open-ended, generic, or recycled assignments beg students to turn in bought, borrowed, or recycled responses.[2]

Also fundamental to the controversial nature of plagiarism detection services today is the recurring question of whether or not the services' use of and replication of students' papers to fill their databases and compare with others constitutes a violation of students' educational privacy or intellectual property rights. In one recent dispute, high school students in Virginia and Arizona filed a joint lawsuit against Turnitin, claiming that the service did not have the right to archive their intellectual property without their permission. Turnitin's legal representatives reportedly claim that its archival practices—saving all submitted papers to be screened for matches against future submissions—fall under the "fair use" designation of legal reproduction of material for educational purposes.[3] The students have disagreed, noting that the addition of their work to the database serves the purpose of a corporation's monetary gain.[4] Accordingly, although as yet none of these services have been deemed illegal, some educators worry that, by using such tools, they may be exposing themselves or their institutions to bad press or even a lawsuit from students or their parents.

A final—for many the most convincing—strike against plagiarism detection services is the degree to which they simply don't work. By and large, these computer algorithms, no matter how well they are designed, *cannot detect plagiarism*—and not just because we can't always agree on its definitions.[5] All these services can detect in the papers they screen, as noted above, are identical sequences of text.[6] Plagiarism detection services cannot detect uncited, and thereby plagiarized, ideas that have been summarized, paraphrased. They cannot detect copy-and-paste plagiarism that students have extensively altered with a thesaurus. They also cannot—nor will they ever be able to—identify whether a paper has been written by a student's roommate, boyfriend, or hired ghostwriter, purchased from a "custom research" paper mill, or recycled for the first time from an offline archive. The only chance teachers have of identifying these types of plagiarism once they have occurred is to be familiar enough with students' writing to recognize a difference when they see it.

Pedagogy, Policing, and Property Rights: So, What Should You Do?

If you decide to use Turnitin in your classes, or if the decision to do so has been made for you, consider the advice below for how to do so in a way that is fair to both you and your students. The following are among the "Recommendations for Academic Integrity and the Use of Plagiarism Detection Services" published by the Intellectual Property Caucus of the Conference on College Composition and Communication (CCCC-IP), under the subheading of instructors' "Roles and Responsibilities":

> In cases where a given institution, college, department, or individual faculty member is committed to using plagiarism detection services, we urge [instructors] to adopt and share practices for responsible, ethical use. At a minimum, such practices include notifying students at the beginning of the term that the [Turnitin] service will be used; providing an opt-out clause; inviting students to submit drafts to the service before turning in final text; and conducting research to discover whether the service is accomplishing what instructors want it to. (CCCC-IP, n.d.)

As the language at the beginning of the above recommendation suggests (and as the rest of the document you may view by visiting the CCCC-IP page, cited in the references below, makes clear), the CCCC-IP does not actively endorse the use of such services, and advises that those who do use them take care. The Academic Integrity Office (AIO) at Syracuse University agrees with the CCCC-IP about the value of "responsible, ethical use," and to that end "strongly recommends" that, if you use Turnitin, you "give students a written statement regarding how you plan to utilize it in your classes." Helpfully, the AIO offers the following suggested language as a "sample statement that you may use or revise to fit your needs":

> This class will be using Turnitin, a plagiarism prevention system. The ease of using the Internet has made it very easy for students to "cut and paste" material into papers that they are writing without proper citation. I will submit all/some papers that you write in this class to Turnitin, a service that identifies "matched text." I will then interpret the originality report, based on your writing capability and writing style. In this class, you will also be given the opportunity to submit your own papers to Turnitin to check that all sources you have used are properly acknowledged and cited. Note that all submitted papers will be included as source documents in the Turnitin.com reference database, solely for the purpose of detecting plagiarism of such papers. (Syracuse University, n.d.)

You might not have the option of allowing students to opt out, or to conduct research on the degree to which the service meets your or your department's desired goals. But in addition to making sure your students understand what you will use the service for and why, you will probably have the opportunity to allow or require students to submit drafts—not just final papers, or in lieu of submitting final papers at all—to the service, so that they can see for themselves whether or not their citation attempts are adequate. If the only "matching" text the site finds is properly bound by quotation marks and its source clearly noted, then students will know that they have successfully avoided at least one type of (often accidental) plagiarism. Through such use, the service can be a way to help students identify problematic citation or source-use practices of their own that they might not be aware of, and can thus be employed as a pedagogical aid rather than merely a policing tool.

No plagiarism detection service, however, should be used—or could ever be effective—as a replacement for good assignment design, clearly communicated expectations, clear skills instruction, varied measures of assessment, and familiarity with students' work: the common denominators of good teaching.

Notes

1. More information about the service itself, as well as usage suggestions and the corporation's official response to controversial topics, is available at http://www.Turnitin.com.

2. For more on how teachers can write assignments that are difficult to plagiarize, see Rebecca Moore Howard's "The Search for a Cure: Understanding the 'Plagiarism Epidemic,'" particularly section 2, "Teachers' roles and responses in Internet plagiarism," available at http://www.mhhe.com/socscience/english/tc/howard/HowardModule03.htm

3. According to the service's "Copyright and Privacy" datasheet, "the documents prepared by Turnitin's legal team from Foley and Lardner" are available at the following link, which was inactive at the time of this writing: http://www.turnitin.com/static/legal

4. News reports about this case are widely available online; see, for example, coverage by *The Washington Post*, *The Chronicle of Higher Education*, or George Mason University's *The Broadside Online*.

5. For example, plagiarism detection services can only detect one of the five types of plagiarism SUNY Geneseo identifies in its quick reference guide for students, available at http://www.geneseo.edu/~brainard/plagiarismtypes.htm.

6. When Turnitin was first released, the software had no way to distinguish between identical sequences that had been properly cited and those that had not been cited at all, nor between students replicating material from others' papers and students replicating material from successive drafts of their *own* papers. Although today's more sophisticated services can recognize quotation marks and block-quote formatting, and with them allow teachers an option to screen only the not-quoted parts of a paper, allowing for fewer "false-positive" identifications of "plagiarized" work, there remains no way for the machine to detect any forms of plagiarism *other* than cut-and-paste copying.

Works Cited

CCCC-IP. (n.d.). CCCC-IP caucus recommendations regarding academic integrity and the use of plagiarism detection service [position statement]. Available at http://ccccip.org/files/CCCC-IPpositionstatementDraft%209%2016%2006.pdf

Syracuse University. (n.d.) Academic Integrity Office—Turnitin information. Available at http://provost.syr.edu/provost/Units/academicprograms/academicintegrity/turnitin.aspx

Turnitin.com. (n.d.). Digital assessment suite [brochure]. Available at http://www.turnitin.com/static/pdf/Turnitin_brochure.pdf

Contributors

Matthew Bertram is a graduate of the State University of New York at Oswego. He received his bachelor's degree in writing arts in 2005 and his master's degree in literature in 2007. His main writing focus is short fiction and poetry. He is not currently employed by any facet of academia, but always manages to find time to write.

Sarah L. Bolton graduated from SUNY Fredonia in 2003 and received her Ph.D. in chemistry from Syracuse University in 2008. While at Syracuse she participated in several research projects involving diruthenium molecular wires in the laboratory of Dr. Michael B. Sponsler and was a teaching assistant for General Chemistry. She is currently a visiting professor at Bucknell University, where she teaches organic chemistry.

David Alan Bozak is the associate dean of the College of Liberal Arts & Sciences at SUNY Oswego. He holds a joint appointment in computer science and psychology and is a recipient of the SUNY Chancellor's Award for Excellence in Teaching. He currently chairs the Committee on Intellectual Integrity at Oswego.

Patrick Drinan is professor of political science at the University of San Diego and was dean of the College of Arts and Sciences, USD, from 1989 to 2006. He is also a past president of the Center for Academic Integrity and holds a Ph.D. in government from the University of Virginia.

Sidney L. Greenblatt is the recently retired senior assistant director for advising and counseling at the Slutzker Center for International Services, serving international students and scholars at Syracuse University and the SUNY College of Environmental Science and Forestry. In addition to holding faculty positions in sociology at both Syracuse and Drew University, Mr. Greenblatt has worked in China, Taiwan, and Hong Kong as an interpreter and specialist on contemporary Chinese society.

David Horacek is finishing his Ph.D. dissertation in philosophy at Syracuse University. In addition to his research on causation, chance, and time travel, David teaches philosophy at SUNY Oswego. He is currently writing the manuscript of a textbook tentatively titled *Critical Thinking for the Information Age*.

Karrie Lamers has earned a bachelor's of science degree in sport management from the University of Wisconsin–La Crosse (UW-L) and is currently pursuing a second undergraduate degree in accounting from UW-L.

Benjamin J. Lovett is an assistant professor of psychology at Elmira College in Elmira, NY. He teaches classes on a variety of topics in psychology, and his research interests include educational assessment, psychiatric diagnosis, and the history of psychology. Ben earned a Ph.D. in school psychology from Syracuse University in 2007.

Patricia MacKown is currently assistant vice president for student development and enrollment services at the University of Central Florida. She has been a member of UCF for 29 years, working in the area of student rights and responsibilities. Ms. MacKown has chaired efforts to develop and implement the UCF Creed as well as initiate ethical decision making opportunities.

Lucy McGregor is an honors student majoring in psychology and geography at the University of Canterbury in Christchurch, New Zealand. Lucy was an undergraduate study-abroad student at Syracuse University in 2006-07, taking courses unavailable to her at Canterbury, such as Religions of the World, Ancient History, and Clinical Psychology. She hopes to continue her studies in a clinical psychology graduate program after graduation.

Michael Murphy is the interim director of college writing and a visiting assistant professor of English at the State University of New York at Oswego. He has published articles on composition theory, cultural studies, and contingent faculty issues.

David Nentwick teaches writing at The College of Coastal Georgia in Brunswick, GA, and is also a Ph.D. candidate in composition and cultural rhetoric at

Syracuse University. His research interests include theories of literacy, critical literacy, ethics and writing, composition and citizenship, writing and the environment, the cultural politics of language, and World Englishes. His dissertation, which deals with writing assessment and curriculum, language policy, identity, and cultural rhetoric, is an ethnographic study of native French speakers in Québec learning academic literacy in English.

James M. Pangborn is adjunct instructor of English at SUNY Oswego and Cayuga Community College, Fulton campus. A long-time nontraditional student, he received his Ph.D. from the University at Buffalo in twentieth-century American literature and continues to cultivate a pragmatist perspective on reading, writing, and teaching. He also writes poems.

Kimberly Ray is a doctoral candidate in child and family studies at Syracuse University. She is currently an early childhood education instructor at Borough of Manhattan Community College.

Amy S. Roache-Fedchenko is a doctoral candidate in the Anthropology Department at Syracuse University. Her archaeological research centers on the role of the blacksmith within fur trading communities in the Great Lakes region. She is a Teaching Fellow with the Future Professoriate Program, and is an FPP Associate for the Anthropology Department.

Ken Sagendorf is the deputy director for faculty development and an assistant professor at the United States Air Force Academy in Colorado Springs, CO, where he mentors new and experienced faculty. He earned his Ph.D. in college science teaching (2007) from Syracuse University, where he worked in the Graduate School with graduate teaching and future faculty preparation programs.

Danielle Schuehler Sherwood is a University Fellow working on her doctorate in chemistry at Syracuse University. She has taught organic and honors general chemistry laboratories and organic chemistry recitation. Danielle has a B.S. in chemistry, with minors in physics, philosophy, and mathematics, from Le Moyne College, where she is currently a member of the alumni association.

Michael Smithee, retired from the Slutzker Center for International Services at Syracuse University, currently uses his experience to consult on international higher education, international education administration, and intercultural training with Smithee Associates. His teaching includes graduate and under-graduate courses on intercultural issues and seminars for Teaching Fellows and teaching assistants on the nature of the intercultural classroom. He was awarded an Ed.D. in higher education from Syracuse University in 1990.

Ruth Federman Stein has a Ph.D. in instructional design, development, and evaluation and an M.A. in English literature. Coauthor of *Using Student Teams in the Classroom* and *Building and Sustaining Learning Communities*, she previously was a teaching consultant, taught in the Syracuse University Writing Program, served on the Syracuse Board of Education, and taught high school English.

Ryan Thibodeau is an assistant professor of psychology at St. John Fisher College in Rochester, NY. He teaches courses in introductory psychology, personality, the psychology of emotion, and history and systems of psychology. He is actively involved in research in the areas of emotion, psychophysiology, and health psychology. Ryan earned his Ph.D. from Syracuse University in 2008.

Tyra Twomey is a part-time editor at Syracuse University's Graduate Editing Center and full-time doctoral candidate in composition and cultural rhetoric. Her dissertation examines the intersection of student writers' use of outside sources with cultural notions of authorship, collaboration, and plagiarism; she has also recently published an article on rhetorical genre.

Brian Udermann is an associate professor in the Department of Exercise and Sport Science and the director of online education at the University of Wisconsin–La Crosse.

Holly White has been a TA for three years while pursuing her Ph.D. in religion at Syracuse University. She has been a Teaching Fellow and was named an Outstanding TA at Syracuse in 2008. Her areas of interest are postmodern and feminist philosophy with special attention to art and justice. Holly received a master's in theological studies from Bethany Theological Seminary in 2004.

Kevin Yee is a faculty developer at the University of Central Florida. Though his Ph.D. is in German, he currently researches classroom teaching and learning methods. His recent publications include an article on best practices for preparing adjunct faculty members to teach at the university, and he also works extensively with graduate teaching assistants.